RICHARD BEN CRAMER

What Do You Think

SIMON &
SCHUSTER

New York London Toronto Sydney Singapore

# of Ted Williams Now?

A REMEMBRANCE

SIMON & SCHUSTER
Rockefeller Center
1230 Avenue of the Americas
New York, NY 10020

Copyright © 2002 by Richard Ben Cramer
All rights reserved, including the right of
reproduction in whole or in part in any form.

Portions of this work first appeared in 1986 in *Esquire*.

SIMON & SCHUSTER and colophon are registered
trademarks of Simon & Schuster, Inc.

For information regarding special discounts for bulk purchases,
please contact Simon & Schuster Special Sales at
1-800-456-6798 or business@simonandschuster.com

Designed by Amy Hill

Manufactured in the United States of America

1   3   5   7   9   10   8   6   4   2

Library of Congress Cataloging-in-Publication Data is available.

ISBN 0-7432-4648-9

All photographs not otherwise credited are reproduced
by permission of AP Wide World Photos.

In the Memory of
CHUCK POWERS

WHAT DO YOU THINK OF TED WILLIAMS NOW?

The young outfielder at Yankee Stadium, May 23, 1941.

TED WILLIAMS

August 30, 1918
July 5, 2002

EVEN IN THE LAST YEARS OF HIS LIFE—even as America and the sub-nation of baseball hungrily re-embraced him—I knew I could provoke surprise (and more than a few arguments) when I said that Ted Williams was not just a great ballplayer, he was a great man.

Reputation dies hard in the baseball nation, and in the larger industry of American iconography. Even at the close of the century, forty years after he'd left the field, there still attached to Ted a lingering whiff of bile from the days when he spat toward booing Fenway fans. And there were heartbroken hundreds who'd freshen that scent with their stories: how he was *rude to them* when they tried to interrupt him for an autograph or a grip-and-grin photo. (The thousands who got their signatures or snapshots found that unremarkable.)

In the northeast corner of the nation, there were still thousands who blamed Ted for never hauling the Red Sox to World Series triumph. (Someone must bear blame for decades of disappointment when their own rooting love was so *piquant* and pure.) . . . Around New York more thousands still resented Ted—and had to reduce him—for contesting with Joe DiMaggio for the title of Greatest of the Golden Age. They insisted that Ted *never won anything* (and reviled him, in short, for never being a Yankee). . . . And westward through the baseball nation—even where the game, not a team, was the passion—historians huffed about his merit (or lack thereof) in left field; the stat-priests essayed talmudic arguments about how many runs he *failed to drive in* (because he'd never swing at a pitch out of the strike zone); and millions of kindly, casual fans (even those who'd agree Ted was the greatest hitter) seemed comfortable if they could tuck him into some pigeonhole—most often as a minor freak of nature: *"Wasn't it true his eyes were twice as good as a normal man's?"* . . .

They missed the point. It wasn't his eyes, it was the avid mind behind them, and the great heart below. Ted was the greatest hitter because he knew more about that job than anyone else. He studied it relentlessly. If you knew anything about it, he wanted to know it—and RIGHT NOW! He ripped the art into knowable shards, which he then could teach with clarity, with conviction (something he was never short on), and with surprising patience and generosity. That's how he was about anything he loved. It was the love that drove him.

Fans couldn't take their eyes off Ted because they could feel his heart yearning with theirs. His want—in his guilelessness he never could hide it—was ratification for theirs. If the coin of his love flipped, and all they could see was rage—still, it was honest currency, for there was no counterfeit in him. Love and rage make a warrior . . . and in the inarticulate gush of words that attended his death in 2002, the particularity of our loss was lost. There were endless rehearsals of his stats, and comparisons to Ruth, Cobb, Gehrig, DiMaggio (of course), Hornsby, Wagner, Mays, Aaron, Barry Bonds . . . there was solemn reference to his service as a pilot in two wars, and speculation on where Ted might have protruded from the great number-pile if he hadn't lost those five prime years . . . there were interviews that seemed intent on reassuring fans that Ted was a nice guy. But he wasn't a nice guy. He was an impossibly high-wide-and-handsome, outsized, obstreperous major-league *overload* of a man who dominated dugouts and made grand any ground he played on—because his great warrior heart could fill ten ballparks. And latterly (here was our loss writ large), he was our link to that time before baseball became just another arm of the entertainment cartel.

I MET TED IN 1986, in service to the entertainment biz: the editors of *Esquire* were scrabbling for features to fit between the ads in an issue the size of a small phone book, entitled "The American Man." And they had the inchoate sense that, somehow, Ted was The American Man. (Problem was, he was a Famously Uncooperative American Man.) So they sent me to meet him. The written product of that encounter—you'll see it in the pages that follow—they ran under the heading: "Mr. Everything."

But I want to spend a minute here on the unwritten product—unwritten because it didn't come clear for years after that publication—what I learned from that meeting with Ted. The big thing was he helped me—when he didn't have to—helped me to see him, understand him, feel with him, and have him in my life. He gave of himself with generosity that he knew would be unrecompensed—and with a fearlessness about his own size that was truly exemplary—that would change my life.

Why didn't I write that? . . . Well, I wrote what I understood. Anyway, I wasn't the story. But, truth be told, it was hard to tell he was helping me, when I'd leave his house all bruised from his insults and half-deaf from his latest loud evidence of how much he knew and I didn't. If I had to sum up what he showed me, it was the difference between *politesse*—Ted wasn't big on that—and what was the large, true-blue, right thing to do.

Here's one small example. In those days, I was a cigarette smoker, which horrified Ted. Not only had he never smoked, he was way ahead of his time in allowing no smoke around him. So if the urge struck, I'd idle through a Camel in his backyard, with its view of the mangroves and the Florida Bay. One day, he was shouting in his living room when the phone rang—he started cursing. (He hated the phone, too.) I only spoke to calm him. "Go ahead, Ted, take the call. I'm goin' out back to have a smoke."

"That smokin'," he growled, "that's the WORST goddamn thing you could do. HOW OLD ARE YOU?"

"Thirty-five."

"WHEN I WAS YOUR AGE, I COULD PULL A TREE OUTA THE GROUND! . . . AN' LOOK AT YOU—LOSIN' YER HAIR!"

IT WAS LATER, too, I understood this was pattern with Ted. He had to rough up the people he meant to help. If you asked him about this, he would answer with a purely tactical truth—in situations where you mean to teach, it's useful to keep clear who knows and who doesn't. But strategically this syndrome was a disaster: as a husband, father, and subject for the sporting press, it brought him unending grief. Ted's old friends couldn't explain it, but they all knew the pattern—and richly enjoyed it. When the old-timers gathered to teach at spring training camp, Bobby Doerr, the erstwhile Sox second baseman, used to grab some young, eager Boston prospect and counsel him to go tell Ted how he meant to swing down on the ball, and tomahawk-chop it for base hits all over the field. Then Doerr and his cronies would watch in glee as Ted erupted in profane abuse all over the child—after which, of course, Ted would spend all day to teach that boy the full theory and practice of hitting (which included, in Ted's view, a slight uppercut).

But it wasn't just hitting, or only Red Sox. At an All-Star Game, World Series, or some other inter-tribal rite, Ted might lavish hours of attention on a hunting-dog confab with Bobby Richardson (who was, for God's sake, *a Yankee*). Apart from the knowledge shared, this was additionally satisfying because Ted could yell at everybody else that they might as well stay the hell away, because he and Bobby were talkin' DOGS—about which they knew NOT A GODDAMN THING! . . . Or Ted might buttonhole some young man—a player of any position, from any team—who wasn't living up to his talent. And in the guise of a talk about hitting, Ted would teach Living Large. He'd tell them, if they would attend to the game—instead of every gonorrheal girl who'd flop on her back, or their antique cars, or those STUPID damn drugs, or those UGLY gold chains, or ferChrist-on-a-crutch-sake PORK-BELLY FUTURES— they could end up with a "MAJOR-LEAGUE NAME" that would be the ticket for "YER WHOLE GODDAMN LIFE!"

None of that ever saw print. For one thing, half of Ted's talk couldn't be printed in a family newspaper. For another, Ted simply wouldn't talk about it. ("WHY THE HELL SHOULD I?") . . . No one ever wrote, for example, that when Darryl Strawberry spiraled out of baseball in a gyre of alcohol, cocaine, and litigious women . . . when his imminent return to the Yankees was sadly scuttled by another acting out—a D.U.I., or getting kicked out of rehab, or something (Straw's woes are hard to keep straight now) . . . the first call he got was not from his lawyer but from Ted Williams, who barely knew him, but who invited Darryl to come live at his house.

This was also pattern with Ted—hiding the generosity of spirit that made him a great man. Maybe he assumed it would be misunderstood. Or worse still, too widely understood. "FerCHRISSAKE! YER MAKIN' ME A DAMN SOCIAL WORKER," he yelled at me one time. This was the fact he wouldn't let me print:

For years, personally and secretly, Ted had been keeping a lot of guys in business—guys too old to qualify for baseball's pension, or they didn't have enough time in the majors, or they didn't have the talent and never made it to the majors—and mostly they were guys too proud to ask, but he knew they were just scraping by. He'd call them up. He'd tell them he was collecting for charity—the Jimmy Fund for kids with cancer, or his museum, something—and they'd hem and haw about how things weren't great with them, just at the moment, might be tough to pitch in. . . ."GODDAMMIT, I CALLED YA!" Ted would bellow into the phone. "SEND ME A CHECK FER TEN BUCKS, SONOFABITCH!" . . . Then, when he got their check with the number, he'd deposit ten grand into their account.

At the finish of the perfect follow-through,
Ted's better-than-perfect eyes would close.

THE FURIOUS SAGA OF
TEDDY BALLGAME

June 1986

FEW MEN TRY FOR BEST EVER, and Ted Williams is one of those. There's a story about him I think of now. This is not about baseball but fishing. He meant to be the best there, too. One day he says to a Boston writer: "Ain't no one in heaven or earth ever knew more about fishing."

"Sure there is," says the scribe.

"Oh, yeah? Who?"

"Well, God made the fish."

"Yeah, awright," Ted says. "But you had to go pretty far back."

IT WAS FORTY-FIVE YEARS AGO, when achievements with a bat first brought him to the nation's notice, that Ted Williams began work on his defense. He wanted fame, and wanted it with a pure, hot eagerness that would have been embarrassing in a smaller man. But he could not stand celebrity. This is a bitch of a line to draw in America's dust.

In this epic battle, as in the million smaller face-offs that are his history, his instinct called for exertion, for a show of force that would *shut those bastards up*. That was always his method as he fought opposing pitchers, and fielders who bunched up on him, eight on one half of the field; as he fought off the few fans who booed him and the thousands who thought he ought to love them, too; as he fought through, alas, three marriages; as he fought to a bloody standoff a Boston press that covered, with comment, his every sneeze and snort. He meant to *dominate*—and to an amazing extent, he did. But he came to know, better than most men, the value of his time. So over the years, Ted Williams learned to avoid annoyance. Now in his seventh decade, he has girded his penchants for privacy and ease with a fierce bristle of dos and don'ts that defeat casual intrusion. He is a hard man to meet.

This is not to paint him as a hermit or a shrinking flower, Garbo with a baseball bat. No, in his hometown of Islamorada, on the Florida Keys, Ted is not hard to *see*. He's out every day, out early and out loud. You might spot him, just after dawn, at a coffee bar where the guides breakfast, quizzing them about their catches and telling them what *he* thinks of fishing here lately, which is, "IT'S HORSESHIT." Or you might notice him in a crowded but quiet tackle shop, poking at a reel that he's seen before, opining that it's not been sold because "THE PRICE IS TOO DAMN HIGH," after which Ted advises his friend, the proprietor, across the room: "YOU MIGHT AS WELL QUIT USING THAT HAIR DYE. YOU'RE GOIN' BALD ANYWAY."

He's always first, 8:00 A.M., at the tennis club. He's been up for hours, he's ready. He fidgets, awaiting appearance by some other, any other, man with a racket, whereupon Ted bellows, before the newcomer can say hello: "WELL, YOU WANNA PLAY?" Ted's voice normally emanates with gale force, even at close range. Apologists attribute this to the ear injury that sent him home from Korea and ended his combat flying career. But Ted can speak softly and hear himself fine, if it's only one friend around. The roar with which he bespeaks himself in a public place, or to anyone else, has nothing to do with his hearing. It's *your* hearing he's worried about.

Ted Williams can hush a room just by entering. There is a force that boils up from him and commands attention. This he has come to accept as his destiny and his due, just as he came to accept the maddening, if respectful, way that opponents pitched around him (he always seemed to be leading the league in bases on balls), or the way every fan in the ballpark seemed always to watch (and to comment on) T. Williams's every move. It was often said that Ted would rather play ball in a lab—where fans couldn't see. But he never blamed fans for watching him. His hate was for those who couldn't or wouldn't *feel* with him, his effort, his exultation, pride, rage, or shame. If they wouldn't share those, then there was his scorn—and he'd *make* them feel that, by God. These days, there are no crowds, but Ted is watched, and why not? What other match could draw a kibitzer's eye when here's Ted, on the near court, pounding toward the net, slashing the air with his big racket, laughing in triumphant derision as he scores with his killer drop shot, or smacking the ball twenty feet long and roaring, "SYPHILITIC MOTHER OF JESUS!" as he hurls his racket to the clay at his feet?

And who could say Ted does not mean to be seen when he stops in front of the kibitzers as he and his opponent change sides? "YOU OKAY?" Ted wheezes as he yells at his foe. "HOW D'YA FEEL? . . . HOW OLD ARE YOU? . . . JUST WORRIED ABOUT YOUR HEART—HA HA HAW." Ted turns and winks, mops his face. A kibitzer says mildly: "How are you, Ted?" And Ted drops the towel, swells with Florida air, grins gloriously, and booms back:

"WELL, HOW DO I LOOK? . . . HUH? . . . *WHAT DO YOU THINK OF TED WILLIAMS NOW?*"

IT IS ANOTHER MATTER, though, to interrupt his tour of life, and force yourself on his attention. This is where matters get tricky—where the dos and don'ts come in. The dos mostly fall to you. They concern your conduct, habits, schedule, attitude, and grooming. It's too long a list to go into here, but suffice it to recall the one thing Ted liked about managing the Washington Senators: "I was in a position where people had to by God *listen.*"

The don'ts, on the other hand, pertain to Ted, and they are probably summed up best by Jimmy Albright, the famous fishing guide, Ted's friend since 1947 and Islamorada neighbor. "Ted don't do," Jimmy says, "mucha anything he don't want to."

He does not wait or bend his schedule: "I haven't got my whole career to screw around with *you,* bush!" He does not screw around with anything for long, unless it's tying flies, or hunting fish, and then he'll spend all night or day with perfect equanimity. He does not reminisce, except in rare moods of ease. He does not talk about his personal life. *"Why the hell should I?"*

His standing in the worlds of baseball and fishing would net him an invitation a night, but he does not go to dinners. One reason is he does not wear ties, and probably hasn't suffered one five times in a quarter century. Neither does he go to parties, where he'd have to stand around, with a drink in his hand, "listening to a lot of bullshit." No, he'd rather watch TV.

He does not go to restaurants, and the reasons are several: They make a fuss, and the owner or cook's on his neck like a gnat. Or worse—it's a stream of *sportsfans* (still Ted's worst epithet) with napkins to sign. At restaurants you wait, wait, *wait*. Restaurants have little chairs and tables, no place for elbows, arms, knees, feet. At restaurants there's never enough food. Lastly, restaurants charge a lot, and Ted doesn't toss money around. (A few years ago he decided that $2.39 was his top price for a pound of beef. For more than a year, he honed his technique on chuck roast and stew meat. Only an incipient boycott by his friends, frequent dinner guests, finally shook his resolve.)

The last reason is seized upon unkindly by restaurateurs in Islamorada and nearby Keys: "No, he doesn't come in. He's too cheap. He'd go all over town, sono-fabitch, and he'd pay by check, hoping they wouldn't cash the check, they'd put it on the wall."

But this is resentment speaking, and it is Ted's lot in life to be misunderstood. Some are put off, for instance, by the unlisted phone, by the steel fence, the burglar alarm, and KEEP OUT signs that stud his gates when he swings them shut, with the carbon-steel chain and the padlock. But friends think nothing of it. A few have his number, but they don't call, as they know he's got the phone off the hook. No, they'll cruise by; if the gates are unchained, if they see his faded blue truck with the bumper sign IF GUNS ARE OUTLAWED ONLY OUT-LAWS WILL HAVE GUNS, if it's not mealtime and not too late and there's nothing they know of that's pissing Ted off, well, then . . . they drive right in.

And this is the way to meet Ted: by introduction of an old friend, like Jimmy Albright. It's Jimmy who knows where to park the car so it won't annoy Ted. It's Jimmy who cautions, as we throw away our cigarettes, that Ted won't allow any smoke in his house. It's Jimmy who starts the ball rolling, calls out "Hiya. Ted!" as the big guy launches himself from his chair and stalks across the living room, muttering in the stentorian growl that passes with him as sotto voce: "Now who the hell is THIS?"

He fills the door. "Awright, come on in. WELL, GET THE HELL IN HERE." He sticks out a hand, but his nose twitches, lip curls at a lingering scent of smoke. Ted's got my hand now, but he says to Jimmy: "S'that you who stinks, or this other one, too? Jesus! Awright, sit down. Sit over there."

Ted wants to keep this short and sweet. He's in the kitchen, filling tumblers with fresh lemonade. Still, his voice rattles the living room: "D'YOU READ THE BOOK?" He means his memoir. *My Turn at Bat.* "Anything you're gonna ask. I guarantee it's in the goddamn book. . . . Yeah, awright. I only got one copy myself.

"Where's the BOOK?" he yells to Louise Kaufman, his mate. Ted thinks that Lou knows the location of everything he wants. "HEY SWEETIE, WHERE'S THAT GODDAMN BOOK?"

Lou has raised three sons, so no man, not even Ted, is going to fluster her. She comes downstairs bearing the book, which she hands to Ted, and which he throws to the floor at my feet. He growls: "Now, I want you to read that. And then I'm gonna ask you a *key question.*"

I ask: "Tomorrow? Should I call?"

"HELL NO."

Jimmy says he'll arrange a meeting.

Ted says: "HOW'S THAT LEMONADE?"

"Good."

"HUH? IS IT? . . . WELL, WHAT DO YOU THINK OF ME?"

In the car, minutes later, Jimmy explains that Ted won't talk on the phone. "Ted gimme his number twenty-five years ago," Jimmy says. "And I never give it yet to any asshole." We both nod solemnly as this fact settles, and we muse on the subject of trust. I'm thinking of the fine camaraderie between sportsmen and . . . wait a minute. Jimmy and Ted have been friends forty years now.

Does that make fifteen years Ted *didn't* give him the number?

I'M GLAD IT'S OVER. Before anything else, understand that I am glad it's over. . . . I wouldn't go back to being eighteen or nineteen years old knowing what was in store, the sourness and the bitterness, knowing how I thought the weight of the damn world was always on my neck, grinding on me. I wouldn't go back to that for anything. I wouldn't *want* to go back. . . . I wanted to be the greatest hitter who ever lived.

—Ted Williams with John Underwood:
My Turn at Bat

San Diego was a small town, and the Williams house was a small box of wood, one story like the rest on Utah Street. It was a workingman's neighborhood, but at the bottom of the Great Depression, a lot of men weren't working. Ted's father was a photographer with a little shop downtown: passport photos, sailors wih their girls; he'd work till nine or ten at night and, still, it wasn't great. Later he got a U.S. marshal's job, in gratitude for some election favors he'd done for Governor Merriam, and that remained his claim to fame. Ted never saw much of him. His mother was the strength in the family, a small woman with a will of steel who gave her life to the Salvation Army. She was always out on the streets, San Diego or south of the border—the "Angel of Tijuana"—out fighting the devil drink, selling the *War Cry* or playing on a cornet, and God-blessing those who vouchsafed a nickel. Sometimes she'd take along her elder boy, and Ted hated it, but he didn't disobey. He was a scrawny kid and shy, and he tried to shrink behind the bass drum so none of his friends would see. There was school, but he wasn't much good there. History was the only part he liked. And then he'd come home, and his mother was out and sometimes it was 10:00 at night, and Ted and his brother, Danny, were still on the porch on Utah Street, waiting for someone to let them in.

Soon home lost its place at the center of Ted's life.

There wasn't much in the little house that could make him feel special. It wasn't the place where he could be the Ted Williams he wanted to be. North Park playground was a block away, and there, with one friend, a bat, and a ball, Ted could be the biggest man in the majors. The game he played was called Big League: one kid pitched, the other hit to a backstop screen. "Okay, here's the great Charlie Gehringer," Ted would announce, as he took his stance. Or sometimes it was Bill Terry, Hack Wilson, or another great man he'd never seen. "Last of the ninth, two men on, two out, here's the pitch . . . *Gehringer swings!*" Ted swung. *Crack!* Another game-winning shot for the great . . . *the Great Ted Williams.*

They were just the dreams of a kid, that's all. But Ted went back to the playground every day. First it was with a friend his own age, then the playground director, Rod Luscomb, a grown man, a two-hundred-pounder who'd made it to the Cal State League. Ted pitched to Luscomb. Luscomb to Ted. At first they'd always tell each other when they were going to throw a curve. But then Ted started calling out: "Don't tell me, just see if I can hit it." *Crack!* Ted could hit it. "Listen, Lusk," Ted used to say. "Someday I'm going to build myself a ballpark with cardboard fences. Then, I'm going to knock 'em all down, every darn one, with home runs." But Ted wasn't hitting many homers with his scrawny chest, those skinny arms. Luscomb set him to push-ups, twenty, then forty, fifty, then a hundred, then fingertip push-ups. Ted did them at home on Utah Street. He picked his high school, Herbert Hoover High, because it was new and he'd have a better chance to make the team. When he made it, he came to school with his glove hung like a badge on his belt. He carried a bat to class. And after his last class (or before), it was back to the playground. Then in darkness, home for dinner, the push-ups, and the dreams.

THERE WERE NO MAJOR LEAGUES in San Diego. There was no TV. He had no more idea of the life he sought than we have of life on the moon. Maybe less, for we've seen the replays. Ted had to dream it all himself. And how could he measure what he'd give up? He wasn't interested in school, didn't care about cars, or money, or girls. He felt so awkward, except on the field. There, he'd show what Ted Williams could do. Now Hoover High went to the state tourney, traveled all the way to Pomona for a doubleheader, and Ted pitched the first game, played outfield in the second, and hit and hit, and Hoover won, and wasn't it great? There was an ice-cream cart, and Ted ate eighteen Popsicles. His teammates started counting when he got to ten. But Ted didn't mind them making fun. That's how good he felt: him hitting, and Hoover winning, and the big crowd. Gee, that's the governor! And Ted found himself in the governor's path, the man who'd tossed his father a job, and he had to say something, and the awkwardness came flooding back, he felt the red in his face. So Ted grabbed tighter on his bat and he barked at Merriam: "HIYA, GOV!" Of course people called him cocky. But he only wondered: Was he good enough?

At seventeen, as high school closed, he signed with the local team, the Coast League Padres. They offered $150 a month and said they'd pay for the whole month of June, even though this was already June 20. So that was Ted's bonus—a hundred bucks—twenty days' pay. He didn't care: he was a step closer, and each day was a new wonder.

He rode the trains, farther from home than he'd ever been. He stayed in hotels with big mirrors, and Ted would stand at a mirror with a bat, or a rolled-up paper, anything—just to see his swing, how he looked. He got balls from the club, so many that his manager, Frank Shellenback, thought Ted must be selling them. No, Ted took them to his playground, got Lusk and maybe a kid to shag flies, and hit the covers off those balls. And he ate on meal money, anything he wanted, until the owner, Bill Lane, called him: "Kid, you're heading the list." And Ted knew he was only hitting .271, so he said, "What list?" Lane growled: "The overeaters list. It's supposed to be $2.50 a day." But Ted was six-three now, and lucky if he weighed 150. He *had* to be stronger. He growled back: "Take it outa my pay."

Best of all, there were major leaguers, real ones, to see. They were old by the time they came to the Coast League, but Ted watched them, almost ate them with his eyes, measured himself against their size. Lefty O'Doul was managing the San Francisco Seals, and he was one of the greats. Ted stopped Lefty on the field one day. He had to know: "Mr. O'Doul, please . . . what should I do to be a good hitter?" And Lefty said: "Kid, best advice I can give you is don't let anybody change you." Ted walked around on air. After that, in bad times, he'd hear O'Doul's voice telling him he'd be okay. The bad times were slumps. If Ted couldn't hit, the world went gray. In his second year with San Diego, Ted hit a stretch of oh-for-eighteen. He hung around the hotel in San Francisco, moping. He didn't know what to do with himself. He got a paper and turned to the sports. There was an interview with O'Doul. The headline said: WILLIAMS GREATEST HITTER SINCE WANER. And Ted thought: I wonder who this Williams is?

IT WAS A NEWSPAPER that told him, too, about Boston buying his contract. The Red Sox! Ted's heart sank. It was a fifth-place club and as far away as any team could be: cold, northerly, foreign. Still, it was big-league, wasn't it?

He had to borrow $200 for the trip east: there were floods that spring, 1938. He got to Sarasota, Florida, about a week late. And when he walked into the clubhouse, all the players were on the field.

"Well, so you're the kid."

It was Johnny Orlando, clubhouse boy. The way Johnny told it, he'd been waiting for this Williams. "Then, one morning, this Li'l Abner walks into the clubhouse. He's got a red sweater on, his shirt open at the neck, a raggedy duffelbag. His hair's on end like he's attached to an electric switch . . . 'Where you been, Kid?' I asked him. 'Don't you know we been working out almost a whole week? Who you supposed to be, Ronald Colman or somebody, you can't get here in time?' " Johnny gave Ted a uniform, the biggest he had in stock. But as Ted grabbed for a couple of bats, his arms and legs stuck out, the shirttail wouldn't stay in the pants.

"Well, come on, Kid." Johnny said, and he led the beanpole out to the field. From the first-base stands, a voice yelled: "Hey, busher, tuck your shirt in! You're in the big leagues now."

Ted wheeled around, face red. "Who's that wise guy up in the stands?" Johnny told him: "That's Joe Cronin, Kid, your manager." Ted put his head down and made for the outfield. It wasn't the reception he'd expected, but at least he had his nickname. Everyone heard Johnny show him around: "Look here, Kid. Go over there, Kid." It stuck right away: it was a role he knew. And soon Joe Cronin would fill the spot Rod Luscomb had held in Ted's life. Cronin was only thirty-one, but that was old enough. He was a hitter and a teacher, a manager, counselor, and Ted was ever the Kid.

Cronin had come from Washington, one of the Red Sox's imported stars. The owner, Tom Yawkey, was buying a contender. Along with Cronin, the Hall of Fame shortstop, Yawkey raided Washington for Ben Chapman, a speedy right fielder and .300 hitter. From the Browns, Yawkey got Joe Vosmik, a left fielder who would hit .324. From the A's, Yawkey bought two old greats, Lefty Grove and Jimmie Foxx, along with Doc Cramer, another .300 hitter for center field.

These were the finest hitters Ted had seen. He couldn't take his eyes off the batter's box. But the presence of all those hitters in camp meant one thing of terrible import to Ted: no nineteen-year-old outfielder was breaking in, not that year, and the veterans let Ted know it. Vosmik, Chapman, and Cramer, rough old boys all of them, made sure he had his share of insults. He lasted about a week, until the club broke camp for the first game in Tampa.

Ted wasn't on the roster for that game. He was

headed to Daytona Beach, where the Minneapolis farm team trained. Ted saw the list and the shame welled up, turned to rage. He yelled to the veteran outfielders: *"I'll be back. And I'll make more money in this fucking game than all three of you combined."* When he walked to the bus stop with Johnny Orlando, he asked: "How much you think those guys make?" And Johnny said: "I don't know, maybe fifteen thousand apiece." Ted nodded, his mouth set in a grim line. He had his salary goal now. Then he borrowed $2.50 from Johnny for the bus trip to the minors.

IN MINNEAPOLIS, Ted led the league in everything: average, home runs, runs batted in, screwball stunts. . . . There were tales of his conduct in the outfield, where he'd sit down between batters, or practice swinging an imaginary bat, watching his leg-stride, watching his wrist-break, watching everything except balls hit to him. If he did notice a fly ball, he'd gallop after it, slapping his ass and yelling. "HI HO SILVER!" He was nineteen, and fans loved him. But if there was one boo, the Kid would hear it, and he'd try to shut that sonofabitch up for good. Once, when a heckler got on him, Ted fired a ball into the stands—and hit the wrong guy. That was more than the manager, poor old Donie Bush, could stand. He went to the owner, Mike Kelley, and announced: "That's it.

One of us goes. Him or me." Kelley replied, quick and firm: "Well, then, Donie, it'll have to be you."

By the time Ted came back to Sarasota, the Red Sox were banking on him, too. They traded Ben Chapman, the right fielder who'd hit .340 the year before. Ted told himself: "I guess that shows what they think of ME." It was like he had to convince himself he was really big-league now. Even after a good day, three-for-four, he'd sit alone in the hotel with the canker of one failure eating at him. If he screwed up, or looked bad, the awkwardness turned to shame, the shame to rage. As the team headed north, Ted was hitting a ton, but it wasn't enough. At the first stop, Atlanta, Johnny Orlando pointed out the strange right-field wall—three parallel fences, one behind the other. Johnny said: "I saw Babe Ruth hit one over that last fence. . . ." Ted vowed right there he'd do it, too. But next day, he couldn't clear one fence. Worse still, he made an error. In the seventh, he put the Sox up with a three-run triple, but it wasn't enough. He had to show what Ted Williams could do! When he struck out in the eighth, he went to right field seething. Then a pop-up twisted toward his foul line. He ran and ran, dropped the ball, then booted it trying to pick it up. Rage was pounding in him. He grabbed the ball and fired it over those right-field walls. By the time the ball hit Ponce de Leon Avenue and bounced up at a Sears store, Cronin had yanked Ted out of the game.

Even Ted couldn't understand what that rage was to him, why he fed it, wouldn't let it go. He only knew that the next day in Atlanta, he smashed a ball over those three walls and trotted to the bench with a hard stare that asked Johnny Orlando, and anyone else who cared to look: Well, what do you think of the Kid now?

HE HAD A GREAT FIRST YEAR in the bigs. On his first Sunday at Fenway Park, he was four-for-five with his first home run, a shot to the bleachers in right-center, where only five balls had landed the whole year before. There were nine Boston dailies that vied in hyperbole on the new hero. TED WILLIAMS REVIVES FEATS OF BABE RUTH, said the *Globe* after Ted's fourth game.

From every town he wrote a letter to Rod Luscomb with a layout of the ballpark and a proud X where his homer hit. He was always first to the stadium and last to leave after a game. He took his bats to the post office to make sure they were the proper weight. He quizzed the veterans mercilessly about the pitchers coming up. "What does Newsom throw in a jam? How about Ruffing's curve?" It was as if he meant to ingest the game. He only thought baseball. On trains, he'd never join the older guys in poker games or drinking bouts. At hotels, it was always room service, and Ted in his shorts, with a bat, at a mirror.

His roomie was Broadway Charlie Wagner, a pitcher with a taste for fancy suits and an occasional night on the town. One night, 4:00 A.M., Wagner was sleeping the sleep of the just when, *wham*, CRASH, he's on the floor, with the bed around his ears, and he figures it's the end. He opens his eyes to see the bean-pole legs, then the shorts, and then the bat. Ted's been practicing, and he hit the bedpost. Does he say he's sorry? No, doesn't say a damn thing to Wagner. He's got a little dream-child smile on his face and he murmurs to himself: "Boy, what power!"

He ended up hitting .327 and leading the league for runs batted in, the first time a rookie ever won that crown. He finished with thirty-one home runs, at least one in each American League park. There was no Rookie of the Year award, but Babe Ruth himself put the title on Ted, and that seemed good enough.

And after the season, he didn't go home. San Diego had lost its hold. His parents were getting a divorce, and that was pain he didn't want to face. He didn't want to see his troubled brother. He didn't want to see the crummy little house with the strained carpet and the chair with the hole where the mice ate through. He had a car now, a green Buick worth a thousand bucks. He went to Minnesota. There was a girl there he might want to see. Her dad was a hunting guide, and Ted could talk to her. And there were ducks to hunt, as many as he wanted. And he could go where he wanted. And do what he wanted. He was twenty-one. And big-league.

EVERYBODY KNEW 1940 would be a great year. Ted knew he'd be better: now he'd seen the pitchers, he knew he could do it. Tom Yawkey sent him a contract for $10,000, double his rookie pay. "I guess that shows what they think of ME."

No one thought about this, but pitchers had seen Ted, too. And this time around, no one was going to try to blow a fastball by him. Cronin was having an off year and Double-X Foxx was getting old and would never again be batting champ. So the pressure fell to Ted. If they pitched around him and he got a walk, that wasn't enough, the Sox needed hits. If he got a hit, it should have been a homer. A coven of bleacherites started riding Ted. And why not? They could always get a rise. Sometimes he'd yell back. Or he'd tell the writers: "I'm gonna take raw hamburger out to feed those wolves." The papers rode the story hard: O Unhappy Star! Then he told the writers: "Aw, Boston's a shitty town. Fans

Before a game, Ted never took his eyes off the pitcher,
searching for any weakness. (Timepix)

are lousy." Now the papers added commentary, pious truths about the Boston fans as the source of Ted's fine income. So Ted let them have it again: "My salary is peanuts. I'd rather be traded to New York." That did it. Now it wasn't just a left-field crowd riding Ted. It was civic sport: *He doesn't like Boston, huh? Who does he think he is?*

Writers worked the clubhouse, trying to *explain* the Kid. Big Jimmie Foxx, a hero to Ted, said: "Aw, he's just bein' a spoiled boy." The great Lefty Grove said if Williams didn't hustle, he'd punch him in the nose. Of course, all that made the papers. Now when writers came to his locker, Ted didn't wait for questions. "HEY, WHAT STINKS?" he'd yell in their faces. "HEY! SOME-THING STINK IN HERE? OH, IT'S YOU. WELL. NO WONDER WITH THAT SHIT YOU WROTE." So they made new nicknames for him: Terrible Ted, the Screw-ball, the Problem Child. Fans picked it up and gave him hell. It didn't seem to matter what he *did* anymore. And Ted read the stories in his hotel room and knew he was alone. Sure, he read the papers, though he always said he didn't. He read the stories twenty times, he'd recite them word for word. He'd pace the room and seethe, want to shut them up, want to hit them back. But he didn't know how.

And Ted would sit alone in the locker room, boning

his bats, not just the handle, like other guys did, but the whole bat, grinding down on the wood, compressing the fiber tighter, making it denser, tougher, harder. He would sting the ball—he'd show them. He'd shut them up. Jesus, he was trying. And he was hitting! Wasn't his average up? Wasn't he leading the league in runs? He was doing it like he'd taught himself, like he'd dreamed. Wasn't that enough? What the hell did they want him to be?

What else could he be? Some players tried to help, to ease him up a bit. Once, Ted gave Doc Cramer a ride, and they were talking hitting, as Ted always did. It was at Kenmore Square that Cramer said: "You know who's the best, don't you? You know who's the best in the league? You are." And Ted never forgot those words. But neither could he forget what was written, just as he couldn't forget one boo, just as he'd never forget the curve that struck him out a year before. Why didn't they understand? He could never forget.

And one day he made an error, and then struck out, and it sounded like all of Fenway was booing, and he ran to the bench with his head down, the red rising in his face, the shame in his belly, and the rage. Ted thought: *These are the ones who cheered, the fans I waved my cap to?* Well, never again. He vowed to himself: *Never again.* And he could not forget that either.

LOU IS IN A MIAMI HOSPITAL for heart tests. Ted says I can drive up with him. He figures we'll talk, and he'll have me out of his hair. We start from his house and I wait for him on the porch, where a weary woman irons. The woman is trying to fill in for Lou, and she's been ironing for hours. Ted may wear a T-shirt until it's half holes and no color at all, but he wants it just so. The woman casts a look of despair at the pile and announces: "She irons his *underpants*."

Ted blows through the back door and makes for the car, Lou's Ford, which he proclaims "a honey of a little car, boys!" When Ted puts his seal of judgment on a thing or person, by habit he alerts the whole dugout. We are out of Islamorada on the crowded highway, U.S. 1, the only road that perseveres to these islets off the corner of the country, when Ted springs his key question. "You read the book? Awright. Now we're going to see how smart YOU are. What would YOU do to start, I mean, the first goddamn thing now, the first thing you see when you're sitting in the seats and the lights go off, how would YOU start the movie?"

Ted is considering a film deal for *My Turn at Bat*. He is working the topic of moviedom, as he does anything he wants to know. Now as he pilots the Ford through Key

Largo, he listens with a grave frown to some possible first scenes. "Awright. Now I'll tell you how it's supposed to start. I mean how the guy's doing it said. . . . It's in a fighter plane, see, flying, from the pilot's eye, over KOREA. Seoul. And it's flying, slow and sunny and then *bang **WHAM BOOOOMMM** the biggest goddamn explosion ever on the screen. I mean **BOOOOOMMM**.* And the screen goes dark. DARK. For maybe ten seconds there's NOTHING. *NOTHING.* And then when it comes back there's the ballpark and the crowd ROARING . . . and that's the beginning."

"Sounds great. Ted."

"Does it? LOOKIT THIS ASSHOLE NOW. I wonder where he's goin'. Well, okay, he's gonna do *that.* Well, okay—I'm passing, too. Fuck it." Ted is pushing traffic hard to be at the hospital by 2:00, when Lou's doctors have promised results from the heart tests. He is trying to be helpful, but he's edgy.

"How long have you and Lou been together?"

"Oh, I've known Lou for thirty-five years. You shouldn't put any of that shit in there. Say I have a wonderful friend, that's all."

"Yeah, but it makes a difference in how a man lives, Ted, whether he's got a woman or not—"

"Boy, that Sylvester Stallone, he's really made something out of that Rocky, hasn't he? . . ."

"So Ted, let me ask you what—"

"LOOK, I don't wanta go through my personal life with YOU, for Chrissake. I won't talk to you about Lou. I won't talk to you about *any of it*. You came down here and you're talkin' about me, as I'm supposed to be different and all that . . ."

"Do you think you're different?"

"NO, not a damn bit. I'm in a little bit different POSITION. I mean, I've had things happen to me that have, uh, made it possible for me to be different. DAMN DIFFERENT in some ways. Everybody's not a big-league ballplayer, everybody doesn't have, uh, coupla hitches in the service, everybody hasn't had uh, as much notoriety about 'em as I had ALL MY LIFE, so . . ."

"So . . ."

"I wanna go NORTH. I'm gonna go up here and go farther down. I made a mistake there. GODDAMMIT, HOW THE HELL DO I GET ON THE FUCKIN' THING? I'll make a U-turn. . . ."

"Ted, I think you were more serious about living life on your own terms. . . ."

"Well, I wanted to be alone at times. It was the hustle and the bustle of the crowd for eight months a year. So sure, I wanted a little more privacy, a little more quiet, a little more tranquillity around me. This is the fucking left we wanted."

"Yeah, but it's not just privacy, Ted. I'm not trying to make it seem unnatural. But what you toss off as a little more privacy led you *off* the continent—so far off in a corner that—"

"Well, lemme tell you about *Koufax*. He got through playin' baseball, he went to a fuckin' little shitty remote town in Maine, and that's where he was for *five years*. Everybody thought he was a recluse, he wasn't very popular just 'cause he wanted to be alone and he finally moved out. Lemme tell you about Sterling Hayward, Hayden. HELL of an actor. And still he wanted to be ALONE, he wanted to TRAVEL, he wanted to be on his BOAT GOIN' TO THE SOUTH SEAS. Christ, uh, look at Hemingway—he went to Key West fifty, sixty years ago. So, see, that's not way outa line! . . . I guess I'll take a right, that oughta do it. Eight seventy-four, do you see 874 anyplace? Go down here till I get to Gilliam Road, or some goddamn thing. . . . Fuck, 874's where I wanted to go, but looked like it was puttin' me back on the fuckin' turnpike—shit. So, you know, seeking privacy and, uh, seeking that kind of thing . . . what road is this?"

"We're on Killian. . . . So privacy, you don't think that's what?"

"*Unusual,* for Chrissake. *Shit.*"

"I don't think it's unusual either."

"WELL, YOU'RE MAKIN' A PROJECT OUT OF IT!"

"No. I don't think it's unusual. . . . You don't think you're exceptionally combative?"

"Nahh, me? Not a bit. Hell, no. THAT SAY KENDALL? Does it? Well, I made a hell of a move here. HELL of a move! See, 874 comes right off there, hospital's down here . . ."

"You're a half-hour early, too."

"Here it is, right here, too. Best hospital in Miami. Expensive sonofabitch, boy. Christ, I'm all for Medicare. And I've always thought that, ALWAYS thought that. Shit. WELL, WHERE ARE YOU GOING? Where ARE you going, lady? *CUNT!*" . . . Ted takes the parking space vacated by the lady and tells me he'll be back in an hour.

WHEN HE COMES BACK he has good news about Lou: all tests are negative, her heart is fine. "Gee, I met the big cardiovascular man, he came in and I met him." Ted sounds twenty years younger.

He's walking to the car when a nurse passes. "GEE, WASN'T IT A SHAME," Ted suddenly booms, "THAT ALLIGATOR BIT THAT LITTLE GIRL'S LEG OFF?" He casts a sly sideward glance at the nurse to see if she's fallen for his favorite joke.

"Honey of a little shittin' car!" he sings out as we hit the road. Now there is no fretting with traffic. Ted makes all the turns. Along the way, he sings forth a monologue about cars, this car, this road, this town of Homestead, that house, his house, the new house he's planning in Central Florida, up on a hill, just about the highest point in the whole goddamn state, what a deal he's getting there, Citrus Hills, HELL of a deal; about his hopes for his kids, his daughter, Claudia, only fourteen, who lives in Vermont with her mother, Ted's third wife, who was too much of a pain in the ass to live with, but gee, she's done a hell of a job with those kids, HELL of a job, the little girl is an actress, she had the lead in the Christmas play, and she was so good the papers up there all said "she bears watching," SHE BEARS WATCHING, and her brother, Ted's boy, John Henry, he's picking colleges now, he's a good boy and Ted's critical, but he can't see too much wrong with that boy, and even the big daughter, Bobby-Jo, she's thirty-eight already, still can bust Ted's chops pretty good, boys, but she's straightening out, now: and these little islands, there's bonefish here, used to be wonderful, years ago, there was *nothing*, NOTHING, except a few of the best fishermen God ever made, and a narrow road between bay and sea, just a little shittin' road, and some women who weren't half bad on the water, or off it either, and the world here was empty and the water was clear and you could have a few pops of rum, maybe get a little horny, go see friends, that's all there was here, a few friends, thirty, thirty-five years ago, when this place was young, when he first fished with Jimmy, and he met Lou. . . .

"Gee, I'm so fuckin' happy about Louise," Ted says. "Goddamn, she's a great person. Have more fun with her than . . . Goddamn."

THEY BOOED IN BOSTON? Well, not in Detroit, the 1941 All-Star Game, with all the nation listening in. Ted doubled in a run in the fourth, but the National League still led 5–3, going into the ninth: then an infield hit, a single, a walk, a botched double play, and here it was: two out, two on, bottom of the ninth: *Here's the Great Ted Williams*. Claude Passeau, the Cubbie on the mound, sends a mean fastball in on his fists. *Williams swings!* When the ball made the seats, Ted started jumping on the base path. DiMaggio met him at home plate, Bob Feller ran out in street clothes. Cronin jumped the box-seat rail, the dugout emptied. The manager, Detroit's Del Baker, kissed him on the forehead. They carried the Kid off the field.

Life magazine's new stop-action equipment caught the beauty
and ferocity of Williams's swing in 1941.

Ted's eyes are locked on the ball to the point of impact.

But after that, the baseball is sent flying by his force—as is
Ted's belt, and his hair, too. (Timepix)

He was showing them all now: after the All-Star break, Ted was still hitting more than .400. Sure, guys hit like that for a month, but then tailed off. No one in the league hit like that for a year, not since the 1920s, and each day the whole country watched. Writers from New York joined the Sox. *Life* brought its new strobe-light camera to photograph Ted in his shorts, swinging like he did in front of the mirror. Ted was on national radio: "Can you keep it up, Kid?" It was murderous pressure. By September, he was slipping, almost a point a day. On the last day, the Sox would have two games in Philadelphia. Ted had slipped to .39955. The way they round off averages, that's still .400. Cronin came to Ted on the eve of the twin bill and offered: "You could sit it out, Kid, have it made." But Ted said he'd play.

That night, he and Johnny Orlando walked Philadelphia. Ted stopped for milk shakes, Johnny for whiskey. Ten thousand people came to Shibe Park, though the games meant nothing. Connie Mack, the dour and penurious owner of the A's, threatened his men with fines if they eased up on Williams. But Ted didn't need help. First game, he got a single, then a home run, then two more singles. Second game, two more hits: one a screaming double that hit Mr. Mack's right-field loudspeaker so hard that the old man had to buy a new horn. In all, Ted went six-for-eight, and .406 for his third season. That night, he went out for chocolate ice cream.

WHO COULD TELL what he'd do the next year: maybe .450, the best *ever*, or break the Babe's record of sixty homers. He got a contract for $30,000, and he meant to fix up his mother's house. He'd have more money than he'd ever expected. He was the toast of the nation. But then the nation went to war.

Ted wanted to play. He'd read where some admiral said we'd kick the Japs back to Tokyo in six months. What was that compared to hitting? A lawyer in Minnesota drew up a plea for deferment, and Ted okayed the request: he was entitled, as his mother's support. When the local board refused deferment, the lawyer sent it up for review by the presidential board. That's when the papers got it. In headlines the size of howitzer shells, they said Ted didn't want to fight for his country. Teddy Ballgame just wanted to play.

Tom Yawkey called to say he could be making the mistake of his life. The league president told Ted to go ahead and play. Papers ran man-on-the-street polls. In Boston, Ted was bigger news than the war in the Pacific. At spring training, Joe Cronin said Ted would be on his own with the fans. "To hell with them," Ted spat. "I've heard plenty of boos." Still, he read every letter—and remembered the venomous ones that said he was an in-grate or a traitor. The one that hurt most said nothing at all: it was just a blank sheet of paper—*yellow* paper.

Opening day in Boston, reporters sat in the left-field stands, out there with soldiers and sailors, to record their reaction to Ted. The Kid treated the day as a personal challenge. His first time up, two on, two strikes, he got a waist-high fastball and drilled it into the bleachers. All the fans rose to cheer, servicemen among them. The Kid was back, and Fenway was with him. "Yeah, 98 percent were for me," Ted said later, as he scraped his bat. A writer said: "You mean 100 percent. I didn't hear a boo." Ted said: "Yeah, they were for me, except a couple of kids in the left-field stand, and a guy out in right. I could hear them."

In May, he enlisted for Navy wings and that shut up most of the hecklers. Still, he was always in a stew of contempt for some joker who said something unfair. It seemed Ted courted the rage now, used it to bone his own fiber. Now there was no awkwardness, no blushing before he blew. It was automatic, a switch in his gut that snapped on and then, watch out for the Kid. One day in July, a fan in left was riding Ted pretty hard. Ted came to bat in the fifth: he took a strange stance and swung late, hit a line drive, but well foul into the left-field seats. Next pitch, again he swung late, hit another liner, but this stayed fair—and Ted didn't run, barely made it to second. Cronin yanked him out of the game, fined him $250 for loafing. But Ted wasn't loafing, the hit caught him by surprise. He'd been trying to kill the heckler with a line drive foul.

TED LOVED THE SERVICE, its certainty and ease. He never had a problem with authority. It was drawing his own lines that gave him fits. He had his fears about the mathematics, navigation problems, and instrument work. But at Amherst College, where the Navy started training, he found his mind was able, and he was pleased.

He loved the feel of an airplane—right from the start. There was coordination in it, and care: those were natural to him. And he was a constant student, always learning in the air. But he was proudest of his gunnery, the way he could hold back until the last pass, then pour out the lead and shred the sleeve. That wasn't study, that was art. He got his wings near the top of his class and signed on as an instructor at Pensacola, Florida. He was happy, and good at his job. Strangely, in uniform, he was freer than before.

On the day he was commissioned (second lieutenant, U.S. Marines), he married that daughter of the hunting guide, Doris Soule from Minnesota. Now, for the first time, he'd have a house, a place on the coast near the base. And now, on off days, he'd scrape up some gas stamps, grab his fly rod, find a lonesome canal, and lose himself in a hunt for snook. Back at the base, Ted would grab a cadet and take him up in his SNJ, and the new guy of course was goggle-eyed—flying with *Ted Williams*—and Ted would make his plane dance over the coast, then he'd dive and point, and yell to the cadet: *"That's where the Kid fished yesterday."*

Orders came through slowly for him. What base commander would give him up as ornament and out-fielder? At last he got combat training and packed up for the Pacific. But Ted was just getting to Hawaii when Japan folded. So he packed up again for Boston, and now he felt he was going to war.

HE CAME BACK like he owned the game. Opening day, Washington, after a three-year layoff: *crack*, a four-hundred-foot home run. And then another and another, all around the league. By the All-Star break in '46, he was hitting .365, with twenty-seven home runs. In the All-Star Game, Ted alone ruined the National League: four straight hits, two homers, and five runs batted in.

And the Red Sox were burying the American League. Tom Yawkey's millions were paying off. The team as a whole was hitting .300, and Ted was hammering the right-field walls. In the first game of two in Cleveland, he hit three homers—one a grand slam when the Sox were behind, the second with two on to tie, the third in the bottom of the ninth to win 11–10. As Ted came up in the second game, Cleveland's manager, Lou Boudreau, started moving men: the right fielder backed toward the corner, center fielder played the wall in right-center; the third baseman moved behind second, and Boudreau, the shortstop, played a deep second base; the second baseman stood in short right, the first baseman stood behind his bag. There were eight men on one half of the field (the left fielder was alone on the other), and Ted stood at home plate and laughed out loud.

There never had been anything like it. He had bent the nature of the game. But he would not bend his own, and slap the ball for singles to left. He hit into the teeth of the Shift (soon copied around the league), and when he slumped, and the Sox with him, the papers started hammering Ted again—his pride, his "attitude." At last, against the Shift in Cleveland, Ted sliced a drive to left-center, and slid across the plate with an inside-the-park home run, first and last of his career. And that won the Sox their first pennant since 1918. But the headlines didn't say, TED HOMERS—or even SOX CLINCH. Instead, eight-column banners cried that Ted stayed away from the champagne party. "Ted Williams," Dave Egan wrote in the *Record,* "is not a team man." And when St.

Louis pulled the Shift in the Series and held Ted to singles, five-for-twenty-five, a new banner read: WILLIAMS BUNTS. And the Red Sox lost that Series, first and last of his career, and after the seventh game, in St. Louis, Ted went to the train, closed his compartment, hung his head, and cried. When he looked up, he saw a crowd watching him through the window. The papers wrote: "Ted Williams cannot win the big ones." The Associated Press voted him number two in a poll for Flop of the Year.

IT SEEMED LIKE TED couldn't laugh anymore, not in a ballpark. He said he was going to Florida to fish. He didn't want to see a bat for months. Soon that was a pattern: one year, before spring training, he tucked in a week in the Everglades. Next year, it was a month. Year after that, longer. In early 1948, the papers discovered that Doris was in a Boston hospital to deliver Ted's first child. But where was the big guy? In Florida? *Fishing?* The mothers of Boston pelted the press with angry letters. "To hell with them," Ted said. He didn't come north for two days. And two days later, he was back fishing. In two years, he'd moved Doris and his daughter, Barbara Joyce, to a house in Miami, the first he'd ever owned. But he never stayed home there either. He heard about some men in the Keys catching bonefish with light fly tackle. When Ted tried this new sport, he found a love that would last longer than any of his marriages.

The Keys were empty, their railroad wrecked by a hurricane in 1935. There were only a few thousand souls on one road that ran for a hundred miles; the rest was just mangrove and mosquitoes, crushed coral islands and shining water. In Islamorada—a town of one store, a bar, a restaurant, a gas pump—some fishing guides, led by Jimmy Albright, were poling their skiffs over shallows that only they knew, hunting bonefish and inventing an art as they went along. These were Ted's kind of men, who'd sneer or scream at a chairman of the stock exchange if he made a lousy cast. Islamorada was a strange meritocracy: if you could not play a fish, tie a fly, cast a line through the wind, you were no one in this town.

Ted could do it all, brilliantly. The guides didn't make much fuss about his fame, but they loved his fishing. His meticulous detail work, always an oddity at Fenway Park, was respected here as the mark of a fine angler. Ted had the best tackle, best reels, best rods, the perfect line, his lures were impeccable. He'd work for hours at a bench in his house, implanting balsa plugs with lead so they'd sail off a spinning rod just so, then settle in the water slowly like a fly. He could stand on the bow of a skiff all day,

Ted was a star at flats-fishing, too—among the first
to catch bonefish with light fly tackle.

watching the water for signs of fish, and soon he was seeing them before the guides. His casts were quick and long, his power was immense. He never seemed to snap a line, never tangled up, his knots were sure, his knowledge grew, and he always wanted to know *more*. He'd question Jimmy relentlessly and argue every point. But if you showed him something once, he never needed showing again. He fished with Jimmy week after week, and one afternoon, as he stood on the bow, he asked without turning his head: "Who's the best you ever fished?" Jimmy said a name, Al Mathers. Ted nodded. "Uh-huh," and asked another question. But he vowed to himself: "He don't know it yet—but the best angler he's had is me."

EVERY WINTER, he'd fish the flats, then head north to make his appearance at the Boston Sportsmen's Show. He'd spend a few days doing fly-casting stunts and then take a couple of hours, at most, to tell Tom Yawkey what he ought to be paid, and pose for pictures as he signed his new contract. His salary was enormous. He was the first to break Babe Ruth's $80,000. Ted didn't care for the money as much as the record. It was history now that was the burr on his back. The joy was gone, but not the dream.

Every day, every season, he was still first to the ballpark, where he'd strip to shorts and bone his bats; still first out to the cage, where he'd bark his imaginary play-by-play: *"Awright, Detroit, top of the ninth . . ."* Then back to his locker for a clean shirt and up at a trot to the dugout, to clap a hostile eye on the pitcher warming up, to pick apart his delivery, hunting for any weakness. No, Ted would not give up on one game, one time at bat, a single pitch. No one since Ruth had hit so many home runs per times at bat. No one in the league hit like Ted, year after year: .342, .343, .369, .343. . . . It seemed he never broke a bat at the plate, but he broke a hundred in the clubhouse runway. If he failed at the plate he'd scream at himself, "YOU GODDAMN FOOL!" and bash the cement, while the Sox in the dugout stared ahead with mute smiles. Once, after a third strike, he smashed the water pipe to the cooler with his bare fists. No one could believe it until the flood began. And on each opening day, Ted would listen to the national anthem and he'd feel the hair rise on the back of his neck, and his hands would clench like they did on the bat, and he'd vow to himself: "This year, the best *ever.*"

In the 1950 All-Star Game, he crashed the outfield wall to catch a drive by Ralph Kiner. His elbow swelled while he played eight innings (and got a single to put his team ahead). The elbow was shattered with thirteen chips off the radius. Surgeons thought he was through, but Ted returned in two months. His first game back, once again: home run, and four-for-four. But Ted could tell as weeks went by that the elbow was not the same. The ball didn't jump off his bat. So all next winter, Ted stayed in the Keys, where he poled a skiff, hunting bone-fish and rebuilding his arm. He was pushing thirty-three now, just coming to know how short was his time. But then, after the '51 season, he was called back to the Marines, drafted for a two-year hitch in Korea. It seemed his time was up.

TED'S LIVING ROOM HAS A WIDE white armchair, into and out of which he heaves himself twenty times a day; the chair has a wide white ottoman onto which he'll flop, as whim dictates, one or both of his big legs. From this chair, he roars commands and inquiries, administering the house and grounds. Across the room, a big TV shows his *National Geographic* specials. At his side, a table holds his reading and correspondence. At the moment, these piles are topped by *Yeager: An Autobiography*, and teachers' reports on his son, John Henry. To Ted's right, ten feet away, there's a doorway to the kitchen, through which Lou can supply him and let him know who that was on the phone. To his left and behind, a grand window affords a view of a patio, his dock, some mangrove, and some Florida Bay. Finally, ahead and to the right, in a distant semicircle, there are chairs and a couch for visitors.

"NOW WE'RE GONNA SEE HOW MUCH *YOU* KNOW, SONOFABITCH," Ted is shouting at Jack Brothers. Jimmy Albright is there, too. The shouting is ritual.

"Ru-mer. R-U-M-E-R." Brothers contends he is spelling the name of the first spinning reel. But Ted has hurled himself up to fetch a fishing encyclopedia, and now he's back in the chair, digging through to the section on spinning. Just so things don't get dull, he says: "Where'd you get that HAIRCUT? D'you have to PAY FOR IT?"

Ted and Jimmy began this colloquy in the early Truman years. Jack helped heat it up when he drifted down from Brooklyn a few years after the war—before Islamorada got its second restaurant or first motel, not to mention the other ten motels, the condos, gift shops, Burger King, or the billboard to proclaim this place: SPORTFISHING CAPITAL OF THE WORLD. These elders are responsible for a lot of the history here, as they helped create flats-fishing and turn it into a sport industry (which they now quietly deplore). Jimmy and Jack were teachers of the first generation of saltwater anglers. Ted is the star of that generation, and its most ferocious pupil.

"Here. HERE! 'Mr. Brown began importing SPIN-NERS, starting with the LUXAR. . . .' THE *LUXAR*. WANNA SEE? GO AHEAD, SONOFABITCH!"

"Yeah, but that don't say the first spinning reel *manufactured*," Brothers grins in triumph. "Sonofabitch, with your books!"

"This is the goddamn HISTORY, Brothers. Not a FUCKING THING about RUMOR, RHEUMER, RHOOOMAN . . . I GUESS YOU DIDN'T KNOW MUCH ABOUT SPINNING REELS, DID YOU?"

Ted is always the one with the books. He wants *answers*, not a lot of bullshit. Ted is always reading history, biography, fact of all kinds. He doesn't like much made of this, as he's tender on the subject of his education. Once in a camp in Africa, while he and his coauthor, John Underwood, gazed at the night sky, Ted turned from the stars and sighed: "Jeez, I wish I was smart like you."

Now he reports to his friends on his college tours with his son, John Henry: "So we get to Babson and I like it. Babson's a pretty good school, boys. HELL of a school, but, uh, they got dorms, boys and girls all in one dorm, see, and I look on the walls and they're written all over, Fuck this and Fuck that. I'm thinking—Gee, right out there on the walls—it just seemed, you know . . ."

"Liberal?" Jimmy suggests.

"Well, I like to see a place with a little more standards than *that*. So we get to Bates. We got this German girl to show us around, see? And she was a smart little shit, two languages, and she's telling us what she's studying, *aw*, a smart little shit! She give us the tour, see, and John Henry loved Bates, LOVED it. We get back to the office and she goes out. I don't know, she musta told someone, told some of her friends, who she just showed around, see? Then somebody *told* her. She didn't know, see. . . .

"Well, a minute later, she's back with some kid and he says, OH, Mr. Williams! and OH this and OH that. And *then* we start talking. And how about *this*, how about *that*, and how would John Henry like to come for a *weekend*, get the feel of the place, you know? . . ."

Ted stops for a moment and thinks to himself. He doesn't really have to finish the thought for his friends, who can see him beaming in his big chair. So he just trails off, to himself:

" . . . Boy mighta thought the old man wasn't gonna . . . you know, around a college. . . . Well!"

THE MAYOR AND THE RED SOX held a day for Ted when he left for flight school. Three weeks into the '52 season, at Fenway, they gave him a Cadillac, and made a donation to the Jimmy Fund, a charity for sick children that Ted supported. They gave him a *Ted Williams Memory Book,* with signatures of four hundred thousand fans. For his last at bat, bottom of the seventh, he gave them a three-run homer to win the game 5–3. He threw a party that night, at his Boston hotel. The crowd was mostly cooks and firemen, bellhops, cabbies, ice-cream men. Ted never liked a smart crowd. Smart people too often asked: "Oh, was your father a ballplayer?" "Oh, what did your mother do?" Ted didn't like to talk about that.

He was just Captain Williams, U.S. Marines, at his flight base at Pohang, Korea. He had a shed for a home and a cot with innertube strips for springs. The base was a sea of mud, the air was misty and cold, and he was always sick. He was flying close air support, low strafing, and bombing runs. His plane was a jet now, an F-9 Panther, but he couldn't take much joy from flying. He was in and out of sick bay. Doctors called it a virus, then pneumonia, but his squadron was short of pilots, so he always flew.

Ted made himself into a warrior pilot—and
a good one in his Marine F-9 Panther jet.

On a bombing run, north of the 38th parallel, Ted lost sight of the plane ahead. He dropped through clouds, and when he came out, he was much too low. North Koreans sent up a hail of bullets. Ted's plane was hit and set afire. The stick stiffened and shook in his hand: his hydraulics were gone. Every warning light was red. The radio quit. A Marine in a nearby F-9 was pointing wildly at Ted's plane. He was trying to signal: "Fire! Bail out!" But Ted's biggest fear was ejecting; at six-three, wedged in as he was, he'd leave his kneecaps under his gauges. So the other pilot led him to a base. Ted hauled his plane into a turn and he felt a shudder of explosion. One of his wheel doors had blown out. Now he was burning below, too. He made for a runway with fire streaming thirty feet behind. Koreans in a village saw his plane and ran for their lives. Only one wheel came down: he had no dive breaks, air flaps, nothing to slow the plane. He hit the concrete at 225 miles an hour and slid for almost a mile, while he mashed the useless brakes and screamed, "STOP YOU DIRTY SONOFA-BITCH STOP STOP STOP." When the F-9 stopped skidding, he somersaulted out the hatch and slammed his helmet to the ground. Two Marines grabbed him on the tarmac, and walked him away as the plane burned to char.

He was flying the next day, and day after. There weren't enough pilots to rest a man. Ted was sicker, weak, and gaunt. Soon his ears were so bad he couldn't hear the radio. He had flown thirty-seven missions and won three air medals when they sent him to a hospital ship. Doctors sent him on to Hawaii and then to Bethesda, Maryland, where at last they gave him a discharge. His thirty-fifth birthday was coming up, he was tired and ill. He didn't want to do anything, much less suit up to play. But Ford Frick, the commissioner, asked him to the '53 All-Star Game, just to throw out the first ball.

So Ted went to Cincinnati, sat in a sport coat in the dugout. Players greeted him like a lost brother; even Ted couldn't hear a boo in the stands. Tom Yawkey was there and Joe Cronin; they worked on the Kid. The league president asked him to come back; the National League president, too. Branch Rickey sat him down for a talk; Casey Stengel put in a plea. Ted went to Bethesda to ask the doctors, and then he told the waiting press to send a message to the fans at Fenway: "Warm up your lungs." He took ten days of batting practice and returned with the Red Sox to Boston. First game, Fenway Park, bottom of the seventh: pinch-hit home run.

.   .   .

TED WILLIAMS was the greatest old hitter. In two months, upon return from Korea, he batted .407 and hit a home run once in every seven at bats. For the next two years, he led the league (.345 and .356), but injuries and walks robbed him of the titles: he didn't get the minimum four hundred at bats. In 1956, he lost the title in the season's last week to twenty-four-year-old Mickey Mantle (who finished with .353 to Ted's .345). The next year, Mantle had an even better season, but Ted, at age thirty-nine, pulled away and won, at .388, more than twenty points ahead of Mantle, more than sixty points ahead of anyone else. With five more hits (say, the leg hits that a younger man would get), it would have been .400. As it was, it stood as the highest average since his own .406, sixteen years before. In 1958, Ted battled for the crown again, this time with a teammate, Pete Runnels. They were even in September, but then, once again, Ted pulled away to win at .328. For the final fifty-five games (including one on his fortieth birthday), he batted .403.

He accomplished these prodigies despite troubles that would have made most men quit. In 1954, he made spring training for the first time in three years, but he wasn't on the field a minute before he fell and broke his collarbone. He was out six weeks and had a steel bar wired into his clavicle. (First day back, twin bill in Detroit: two home runs, eight-for-nine, seven RBIs.) In 1955, Doris alleged in divorce court that he'd treated her with "extreme cruelty" and constant profane abuse. Boston papers ran the story under two-inch headlines: TED GETS DIVORCE, with a "box score" on the money, the house, the car, and "Mrs. Ted's" custody of Bobby-Jo. In 1956, Ted came forth with his Great Expectorations. In a scoreless game with the Yankees, in front of Fenway's biggest crowd since World War II, he was booed for an error, and he let fans know what he thought of them: he spat toward the right-field stands and spat toward the left, and when fans rained more boos on his head, he leaped out of the dugout and sprayed all around. "Oh, no, this is a bad scene," Curt Gowdy, the Sox broadcaster, mourned to his microphone. Tom Yawkey heard the game on radio, and Ted got a $5,000 fine (tying another Babe Ruth record). Boston writers said Ted ought to quit. But Ted was in the next game, Family Night, and at his appearance, fans gave him a five-minute ovation. (He then hit a home run in the bottom of the eighth and clapped his hand over his mouth as he scored the winning run.) In 1957, grippe knocked him flat and stuck him in his hotel for seventeen days in September. He came back to hit four consecutive home runs. In 1958, ptomaine from bad oysters wrecked opening day, then he injured an ankle, pulled a muscle in his side, and hurt his wrist twice. In September, after a called third strike, Ted threw his bat and watched in horror as it sailed to the stands and clonked a gray-haired lady on the head. Ted sat in tears in the dugout and had to be ordered to his place in left field. But over the next twenty at bats, he hit .500.

Now the switch in his gut was always on. The Red Sox gave him a single room and barred the press from the clubhouse for two hours before each game. But it wasn't outside annoyance that was fueling Ted's rage. He'd wake up in the middle of the night, screaming obscenities in the dark. He kept himself alone and pushed away affection. There were plenty of women who would have loved to help. But Ted would say: "WOMEN?" and then he'd grab his crotch. "ALL THEY WANT IS WHAT I GOT RIGHT HERE." Now the press didn't cover just explosions on the field. The *American* wrote him up for shredding a telephone book all over the floor when a hotel maid failed to clean his room. "Now tell me some more," wrote Austen Lake, "about Ted's big, charitable, long-suffering spirit." Roger Kahn reported a scene when Ted was asked about Billy Klaus, the shortstop who was coming back after a bad year. "You're asking

Ted regarded reporters—"The Knights of the Keyboard,"
he called them—with the same baleful wariness he
showed toward pitchers. (Timepix)

ME about a BAD YEAR? . . . OLD T.S.W., HE DON'T HAVE BAD YEARS."

But old Ted had a terrible year in 1959. A pain in his neck turned to stiffness, and he was in traction for three weeks. When he came out, he could barely look at the pitcher. His average languished below .300 for the first time in his career. For the first time, he was benched for not hitting. The sight of the Kid at the plate was pathetic; even the papers softened. They started summing up his career, treating him like an old building menaced by the wrecking ball. He finished at .254 and went to see Tom Yawkey. "Why don't you just wrap it up?" Yawkey said, and Ted started to boil. No one was going to make him retire. Ted said he meant to play, and Yawkey, who loved the Kid, offered to renew his contract: $125,000, the highest ever. No, Ted said, he'd had a lousy year and he wanted a cut. So Ted signed for $90,000 and came back one more time.

Opening day, Washington: a five-hundred-foot home run. Next day, another. He slammed his five-hundredth in Cleveland. He was past Lou Gehrig and then Mel Ott. Only Foxx and Ruth would top him on the all-time list. At forty-two, Ted finished his year with twenty-nine homers and .316. Talk revived that Ted might be back. But this was really quits. On his last day at Fenway, a headline cried: WHAT WILL WE DO WITHOUT TED? And though the day was dreary and the season without hope, ten thousand came out to cheer him and hear him say goodbye. There was another check for the Jimmy Fund and, this time, a silver bowl. And Ted made a speech that said, despite all, he felt lucky to play for these fans. And when he came up in the eighth and they stood to cheer, he showed them what Ted Williams could do. He hit a Jack Fisher fastball into the bullpen in right field. And he thought about tipping his cap as he rounded first, but he couldn't—even then, couldn't forget . . . so he ran it straight into the dugout, and wouldn't come out for a bow.

NOW IT WAS NO HOBBY: Ted fished harder and fished more than any man around. After his divorce from Doris, he'd made his home in Islamorada, bought a little place on the ocean side, with no phone and just room for one man and gear. He'd wake before dawn and spend the day in his boat, then come in, maybe cook a steak, maybe drive off to a Cuban or Italian joint where they served big portions and left him alone. Then, back home, he'd tie a few flies and be in bed by 10:00. He kept it very spare. He didn't even have a TV. That's how he met Louise. He wanted to see a Joe Louis fight, so Jimmy

With sadness—and with thanks—Williams said goodbye to the fans at Fenway before his last game, September 28, 1960.

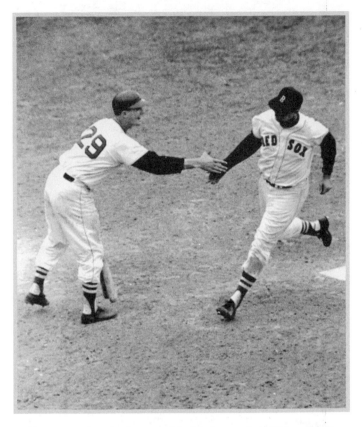

But even when he homered in his last at-bat, Ted couldn't forgive or forget—head down, hat firmly in place, he ran it straight into the dugout and wouldn't come out for a bow.

took him to Lou's big house. Her husband was a businessman from Ohio, and they had a TV, they had everything. Lou had her five kids, the best home, best furniture, best car, and best guides. Though she wasn't a woman of leisure, she was a pretty good angler, too. She could talk fishing with Ted. Yes, they could talk. And soon, Lou would have a little money of her own—an inheritance that she'd use to buy a divorce. She wanted to do for herself, she said. And there was something else, too: "I met Ted Williams," Louise said. "And he was the most gorgeous thing I ever saw in my life."

Now Ted's life was his to make, too. He signed a six-figure deal with Sears, to lend his name to their line of tackle, hunting gear, and sporting goods. Now, when Hurricane Donna wrecked his little house on the ocean, he bought his three-bedroom place on the bay, near Louise's house. Now he bought a salmon pool on the Miramichi, in New Brunswick, Canada, and he fished the summer season there. In Islamorada, he was out every day, fall, winter, spring. He wanted the most and the biggest—bonefish, tarpon, salmon—he called them the Big Three. He wanted a thousand of each, and kept books on his progress. He thought fishing and talked fishing and taught fishing at shows for Sears. He felt the joy of the sport, still. But now there was something else: the switch that clicked when he'd get a hot fish that ran and broke off his lure: Ted would slam his rod to the deck, or break it in half on the boat. "HERE, YOU LOUSY SONOFABITCH . . ." He'd hurl the rod into the bay. "TAKE THAT, TOO."

He married again in 1961, a tall blond model from Chicago, Lee Howard. They'd both been divorced, and they thought they'd make a go. Ted brought her down to the Keys. But he still wasn't staying home: he'd be out at dawn without a word on where he'd go, or what he planned, and then he'd come home, sometimes still without words. Sometimes there was only rage and Lee found she was no match. After two years, she couldn't take it. She said: "I couldn't do anything right. If we went fishing, he would scream at me, call me a ——— and kick the tackle box."

So Ted found another woman, one to meet him, fire with fire. Her name was Dolores Wettach, a tall, large-eyed, former Miss Vermont. He spotted her across the aisle on a long plane flight. He was coming home from fishing in New Zealand. Dolores had been in Australia, on a modeling assignment for *Vogue*. He wrote a note: "Who are you?" He wadded it up, tossed it at her. She looked him over, tossed one back: "Who are *you*?" He tossed: "Mr. Williams, a fisherman," and later told her his first name was Sam. It wasn't until their third date that she found out he'd done anything but fish. When he found out she was a farm girl who loved the outdoors as much as he, he figured he'd met his match. In a way, he had. She learned to fish, she could hunt, she could drink, she could curse like a guide. And when they fought, it was toe to toe, and Ted who slammed out of the house. They had a son, John Henry, and daughter, Claudia. But that didn't stop the fights, just as it hadn't with Bobby-Jo, the daughter he'd had with Doris. Ted would tell his friends he wasn't cut out for family. He was sick at heart when Bobby-Jo left school and didn't go to college. He would seethe when any woman let him know that he'd have to change. What the hell did they want? When Dolores became his third divorce, Ted was through with marriage.

TED MADE THE HALL OF FAME in 1966. His old enemies, the writers, gave him the largest vote ever. So Ted went north to Cooperstown, and gave a short speech outside the Hall. Then he went back to Florida. He never went inside. They gave him a copy of his plaque. It listed his .406 year, his batting titles, slugging titles, total bases, walks, home runs. It didn't say anything about the wars, the dream, the rage, the cost. But how much can a plaque say?

There are no statistics on fans, how they felt, what they took from the game. How many of their days did Ted turn around? How many days did he turn to occasions? And not just with hits: there was a special sound from a crowd when Ted got his pitch, turned on the ball, whipped his bat in that perfect arc—and missed. It was a murmurous rustle, as thousands at once let breath escape, gathered themselves, and leaned forward again. To see Ted suffer a *third* strike was an event four times more rare, and more remarkable, than seeing him get a hit. When Ted retired, some owners feared for attendance *in the league*. In Boston, where millions came through the years to cheer, to boo, to care what he did, there was an accretion of memory so bright, bittersweet, and strong that when he left, the light was gone. And Fenway was left with a lesser game.

And what was Ted left with? Well, there was pride. He'd done, he believed, the hardest thing in sport: by God, he hit the ball. And there was pride in his new life: he had his name on more rods and reels, hunting guns, tackle boxes, jackets, boots, and bats than any man in the world. He studied fishing like no other man, and lent

Casey Stengel and Ted display their new plaques at the
Cooperstown Hall of Fame, July 26, 1966.

to it his fame and grace, his discerning eye. He had his tournament wins and trophies, a fishing book and fishing movies, and he got his thousand of the Big Three. Jimmy Albright says to this day: "Best all around, the best is Ted." But soon there were scores of boats on the bay and not so many fish. And even the Miramichi had no pools with salmon wall to wall. And Ted walked away from the tournaments. There wasn't the feeling of sport in them, or respect for the fish anymore. Somehow it had changed. Or maybe it was Ted.

Last year, Ted and Lou went up to Cooperstown together. This was for the unveiling of a statue of the Kid. There are many plaques in the Hall of Fame, but only two statues: just the Babe and him. And Ted went into the Hall this time, pulled the sheet off his statue and looked at his young self in the finish of that perfect swing. He looked and he looked, while the crowd got quiet, and the strobes stopped flashing. And when he tried to speak, he wept.

"**H**EY WHERE THE HELL IS HE?" It's after 4:00, and Ted's getting hungry. "I'M GONNA CALL HIM."

Lou says, "Don't be ugly."

"I'm not ugly," Ted insists, but quietly. He dials, and bends to look at me. "Hey, if this guy doesn't come, you can eat. You wanna eat here?" Then to the phone: "WHERE THE HELL ARE YOU?"

"Ted, don't be mean."

"I'm not. YEAH, TOMORROW? WELL OKAY, BUDDY." Ted has had a successful phone conversation. Quick, and to the point.

"Awright, you can eat. Hey, sweetie, take him up so he can see."

There are no mementos in the living room, but Lou has put a few special things in a little room upstairs. Most of the pictures have to do with Ted, but the warmth of the room, and its character, have to do with Louise. This is no shrine. It is a room for right now, a room they walk through every day, and a handsome little place, too. Now it is filled with her quiet energy. "Here's Ted Williams when I met him," she says. "And if that isn't gorgeous, I'll eat my hat." And here's an old photo of Lou in shorts, with a fly rod, looking fragile next to a tarpon she pulled from Florida Bay. She does not seem fragile now. She is spry and able. She has been with Ted ten years straight, and that speaks volumes for her strength and agility. She gets angry sometimes that people do not credit Ted with tenderness—"You don't know him," she says, and her voice has a surprising edge—but she also knows he'll seldom show it. So here she shows a lonely young Ted with a little suitcase, off to flight school. Here's Ted and Tom Yawkey, and look: Mr. Yawkey has pictures of Ted behind him, too. "Here he is in Korea," says Louise. "You know, when he landed that plane, the blood was pouring from his ears. I have to tell people that . . . because he's *so* loud. Big, too." Lou picks up a cushion of a window seat. There are pictures beneath. "See, he's done so many things. . . ."

"Hey, you want a drink?" Ted is calling. "TED WILLIAMS IS GONNA HAVE A DRINK."

Soon he flops into his chair with a tumbler, and hands over a videotape. He wants it in the VCR. He says: "This is the most wonderful guy. Hell of a guy. Bill Ziegler. I got him into the majors. . . ." That was when Ted came back in '69 to manage the Senators. Bill Ziegler was the trainer.

"So he had a son and he named him Ted Williams Ziegler. You're gonna see him now. IS IT IN? HEY, YOU LISTENING?" The tape shows Ziegler's two sons batting. Ziegler sends the tapes for analysis. The soundtrack sends out a steady percussion: *thwack . . . thwack . . . thwack*. Both boys get wood on the ball. "I'm gonna show you the first tape he sent, and I'm gonna ask what's the difference. See this kid, I told him his hips, he's got to get them OPEN."

From the kitchen, Lou protests: "Ted! Not now. Wait for me!"

"SEE? . . ." *Thwack*. "Ground ball. A little slow with his hands."

From Lou: "Okay, okay, I don't know nothin'."

"HANDS THROUGH!" *Thwack*. "Center field, always to center, see where his hips are pointed? He's got to [*thwack*] OPEN 'EM UP."

From Lou, coming in, wiping her hands as she watches: "He doesn't step into it like Ted Williams."

Ted pretends he doesn't hear. "Hips come through OPEN. . . ."

"He doesn't bring his hands around like you do, honey."

"Yeah, he's got to, GROUND BALL! See, when I'M up"—and now Ted takes his stance in the living room—"I'm grindin'. . . ." Now his hands are working. "I got the hands cocked. COCKED!" And here's the pitch. "BAMMMM!" says Ted, as he takes his cut and asks: "We got Bill Ziegler's number? WHERE'S HIS NUMBER?"

Ted is yelling on the phone in the kitchen, and Lou is

in the living room, fitting her thoughts to small silences.
"When Ted talks [*thwack*] it's always right now. . . ."

"BILL, I WANNA SEE HIM ON HIS FRONT FOOT
MORE, AND THE HANDS QUICK, *QUICK*. . . ."

"You know, the baseball players . . . it's not macho,
they're just . . . athletes, just beautiful boys. . . ."

Ted hangs up and throws himself into his chair:
"AWRIGHT, MAJOR LEAGUE! LET'S SET IT UP." That
means dinner. Lou's cooking Chinese. Ted's still watching Ziegler's kids. "Ground ball. You don't make history
hittin' 'em on the ground, boys." Now he pulls away
from the TV. "Sweetie," he sings playfully. "We got any
sake-o?" Lou sings: "Not tonight-eo." Ted sings: "Well,
where's the wine-o?"

Lou says grace while all hold hands. Then we set to
food, and Ted is major-league. "It's good, huh?" he says
between mouthfuls. "Well, isn't it? HEY! Aren't you
gonna finish that rice?"

He's finished fast and back in his chair. "We got any
sweets?"

A little album on the coffee table has pictures from
Christmas. John Henry gave his letter of acceptance
from Bates as his present to Ted. It's got Ted thinking
now about the car he's got to buy so John Henry can take
a car to school. "Got to have a car . . ." He's thinking

aloud so Louise can check this out. "'Course, there's gonna have to be rules. . . ." He's working it over in his mind, and he muses: "Maybe say that other than school . . . he can't take the car if his mother says no. . . ." Lou is in a chair across the room. She's nodding. "HAVE to be rules," Ted says, "so he doesn't just slam out of the house . . . slam out and JUMP IN THE CAR. . . ."

Something has turned in his gut, and his face is working, growing harder. There's a mean glitter in his eye, and he's thinking of his elder daughter, walking away from him. . . .

"SLAM   OUT . . . LIKE   MY   DAUGHTER   USED TO . . ."

His teeth are clenched and the words are spat. It's like he's turned inward to face something we cannot see. It is a fearsome sight, this big man, forward, stiff in his chair, hurling ugly words at his vision of pain. . . . I feel I should leave the room, but too late.

"*. . . THAT BURNED ME . . .*"

The switch is on. Lou calls it the Devil in him.

"*. . . A PAIN IN MY HAIRY RECTUM!*"

"Nice," says Lou. She is fighting for him. She has not flinched.

"Well, DID," he says through clenched teeth. "AND MAKES YOU HATE BROADS! . . ."

"Ted. Stop." But Ted is gone.

" . . . HATE GOD! . . ."

"TED!"

" . . . *HATE LIFE!*"

"TED! . . . JUST . . . STOP!"

"DON'T YOU TELL ME TO STOP. DON'T YOU *EVER* TELL ME TO STOP."

Lou's mouth twists up slightly, and she snorts: "HAH!"

And that does it. They've beaten it, or Lou has, or it's just gone away. Ted sinks back in his chair. His jaw is unclenched. He grins shyly. "You know, I love this girl like I never. . . ."

Lou sits back, too, and laughs.

"SHE'S IN TRAINING," Ted says. "I'M TEACHIN' HER. . . ."

"He sure is," Lou says, like it's banter, but her voice is limp. She heads back to the kitchen, and Ted follows her with his eyes.

Then he finds me on his couch, and he tries to sneer through his grin: "WHEN ARE YOU LEAVING? HUH?

" . . . JESUS, YOU'RE LIKE THE GODDAMN RUSSIAN SECRET POLICE!

" . . . OKAY, BYE! YEAH, SURE, GOODBYE!"

Ted walks me out to the driveway. As I start the car, Lou's face is a smile in the window, and Ted is bent at his belly, grabbing their new dalmatian puppy, tickling it with his big hands while the dog rolls and paws the air. And as I ease the car into gear, I hear Ted's voice behind—cooing, very softly now: "Do I love this little dog, huh? . . . Yes, this little shittin' dog . . . Yes, yes, I love you . . . Yes, I do."

LATE LOVES

IN THE LATTER HALF OF HIS LIFE, after he left Fenway Park—not the gaudiest years, but in some ways his best—Ted Williams found love. Or he learned to recognize the love that was in him. And he let it out.

This process was gradual—played out in private and difficult, as hitting never was—but to my mind as inspiring as his young quest toward his first ambition: to be the greatest hitter who ever lived.

And unlike baseball (where the best advice Ted ever got was, "Kid, don't let anybody change you") . . . in this process, he had to change—and he found someone who could offer real help. That was Louise Kaufman, who was most often described as Ted's "special friend" or "longtime companion," but was in fact the love of his life.

When I first wrote about them, I only hinted at her story: how, after she bought her divorce to be with Ted Williams, she had to suffer through two more of his knucklehead marriages . . . but she hung in there, she got her man. And when she did, it was Louise who would not wed—for she knew him, and the way marriage flipped his switch, prodded him to trapped-animal combat. She knew him and *would not fear him*: he'd met his match in bravery. For though she was about half his size, as quiet as he was loud, she dwarfed him in faith— and faith in him.

It was Louise who helped Ted to face the one thing he ever feared—his failures. And in particular, she steered him, aided him, egged him, to make a new place in his life for his kids. It wasn't that they were failures—not in his eyes—but he always felt he had failed them. He used to say, late in life, with characteristic volume and candor: "Yeah, I could do a lot of things. But I was horseshit as a father, boys—HORSESHIT!" He tried to make amends.

His elder daughter, Barbara Joyce—Bobby-Jo, the only child of his first marriage, and a spur to Ted's anger for so many years—he now invited to come and live by him. For her new home, he gave her a parcel of land that he owned, less than a mile from his new house at Citrus Hills, in West Central Florida. And then her two daughters—Ted's first grandchildren—became his new visitors, and his life's new delight.

His younger daughter, Claudia, child of his third marriage, proved to be more cussedly independent (which trait Ted now said he admired, and tried not to rage at—she came by it honestly, after all). He was proud of her: she was beautiful, and bright—Ted helped with college, and she went through *in three years,* which included a stint at a university in Germany—and of course, she spoke German, as Ted said, *perfect!* (Yeah, a SMART little shit!) . . . In latter years, he'd call her home in St. Petersburg, and woo her, ask her to drive out and visit him. Why? So he could tell her he loved her! "CHRISSAKE," Ted would say, when he'd hung up the phone. "SHE HAS TO KNOW THAT! THAT'S IMPORTANT, GOD-DAMMIT!"

But of all the kids it was his son, John Henry—also from his third marriage—who became closest to his dad. As a matter of fact, he moved in on his dad. When Louise Kaufman's heart gave out and she died, in 1993, it was John Henry who came to Citrus Hills, and in short order took over Ted's life. The old man needed help—that much was clear. He was bereft without Louise. And he'd already suffered his first stroke, which diminished his vitality, mobility—and his famous eyesight. Still, the advent of John Henry was a much-mixed blessing.

All the kids had received memorabilia from Ted—autographed pictures, balls, and especially bats—that could make them millionaires. But John Henry, who'd been to business school in Maine, had bigger ideas. He meant to turn Ted's signature, and Ted, into an industry. Even as his father had a second stroke, and then a third, John Henry kept Ted signing—bats, balls, shirts, caps. . . . In the words of Ted's former manager of household, Kay Munday: "Sign, sign, sign. They would do it for hours at a time until the man was so tired he couldn't write anymore. He pushed and pushed his dad . . . and of course it was for money. The ultimate thing was money." That was the ultimate for John Henry. Ted was never crazy for money—enough was enough. And as for the meat-market autograph business, Ted purely reviled it. But with his son he was compliant.

He wasn't going to turn away from the kid, now. He'd done enough of that when the boy was young. Even when John Henry would erupt in rage *at Ted* (often for giving away stuff the new Web site might have sold), the old man tended to blame himself. . . . Even when the boy fought with his sisters (he sued Claudia for trying to sell the bats Ted gave her), and made ugly accusations

against Louise's kids—*and Louise* . . . even as the boy of-
fended Ted's admirers, and dismissed the workers who
took care of Ted's health and home (he accused them of
stealing autographed items) . . . even after John Henry's
businesses fell apart in lawsuits, bad loans, bankruptcy
. . . Ted looked for reasons to admire the kid. "There's
my son now," Ted would say, as John Henry slammed
into the house at Citrus Hills. "Lookit 'im—he's a big
handsome bastard—isn't he? WELL, ISN'T HE?" . . .
Ted knew something about big, angry, handsome young
bastards. And by that time, he was in love with the idea
of loving his son.

HE FELL IN LOVE with showing his friends that he loved
them. The urge grew more poignant and pressing as he
lost them to old age—he outlived so many in his generation. When he lost his old Florida Bay fishing-guide
buddies, Jimmy Albright and Jack Brothers—and then,
too, his north-woods fishing companion, the Maine
newspaperman Bud Leavitt—Ted fretted that he might
not have told them well enough, often enough, how
much they meant to him. So he'd call up their kids—
apropos of nothing in particular: "You know, I loved
your dad—LOVED 'IM!"

In this, too, Ted found help—from one of the oldest
friends he had. Bob Breitbard and Ted went back (nearly

three quarters of a century!) to Hoover High School in San Diego, where Breitbard played football, while Ted was the star of the baseball team. But they came from very different homes: the Breitbards were close and comfy, huggers and smoochers, the way Ted's folks never were. So, when they were still friends as old men—they had visited back and forth, east and west coast; they had traveled together, talked hours on the phone; Breitbard had enshrined Ted in his San Diego Hall of Champions, and contributed to Ted's museum and Hitters Hall of Fame in Hernando, Florida . . . Breitbard said goodbye, one time, by telling Ted he loved him, and planting a kiss on Ted's cheek. Ted reeled back, almost fell off his chair. But Bob stuck his face close again, and said: "Go ahead. You kiss me now, too." Ted did. After that, they never saw each other, or got off the phone, without the big words: "I love you."

And after that, Ted brought to this new art his old, accustomed passion for practice. Friends from his team—he'd fly across the country to be with Bobby Doerr, or he'd drive the length of Florida to the winter home of Dom DiMaggio—so he could tell them he loved them. Even after his strokes (and a fall that yielded a broken hip) put him in a wheelchair and made travel difficult, Ted would push himself for friends he too seldom saw. There was his old Marine Corps colleague ("a HELLUVA flier, boys"), John Glenn—who was a bit pinned down himself, with duties in the Senate and space program . . . or another old outdoorsman—they'd fished together in Alaska and Russia—Bobby Knight, the basketball coach. (Another man misunderstood: Ted didn't care what anybody said of him. *Mother-o'*-JEEZUS, I LOVE THE SONOFABITCH.")

But it wasn't just old friends or famous ones. Ted made new ones all the time, now. Just a few years before his death, when he toured Boston's Dana-Farber Cancer Institute, Ted rolled in his chair through a hero's welcome: doctors, nurses, young patients and their parents, orderlies, aides—seemed like a thousand people, lining the hallways, clapping and cheering his progress—he'd raised so many millions for the Jimmy Fund that financed their hospital. But Ted was so excited to meet *them*—the doctors, especially—he wanted them to know, he LOVED what they did, LOVED THEM . . . and when they'd thank him, he'd say: they were the heroes.

Most of all, it was for the patients, the kids—Ted let it all out. He'd wheel into a ward and straight for some parents who were holding their child, suffering with cancer. Ted would gently set his big paw onto the little bald head and announce: "THIS KID'S GONNA MAKE IT. I GUARANTEE IT!" Or he'd sit with a couple of kids, and guess their ages—he wasn't bad at that, he'd amaze them: *How'd he know that?* . . . "Oh, I know these things. AND I KNOW YOU'RE GONNA GET BETTER! You do what the doctor says—YOU PROMISE?"

In the old days, it was often written that Ted always mourned his brother, Danny, who died from leukemia in 1960, which was the year Ted retired from the Red Sox. They wrote, that was why Ted supported the Jimmy Fund, or why he'd call the house of perfect strangers, to yell encouragement to their child through the phone. For the love of Danny—so it was said—Ted would do anything for kids with cancer. But that wasn't strictly true. For one thing, Ted lent his name and fame to the Jimmy Fund for almost a decade before he retired. And by the end—when he'd worked for the benefit of sick kids for nearly fifty years—it was clear, at least to him, that it wasn't for Danny, it was for Ted. Any kid in pain was his friend.

When Ted moved into his new place at Citrus Hills, he soon found there was a young girl, a neighbor named Tricia. She'd been paralyzed. Ted called her right up. He invited her to come to his house—bring her mom, or the girl who took care of her in the daytime—and use his pool. So, Tricia came. Then he called her again. Then he called her every couple of days—*Wasn't she comin' to use the pool? What the hell did he have that pool for?* (Ted would never go in himself.) . . . So, she came all the time. And when she did, he'd wheel right out in *his* chair—and they'd talk, he'd command the staff to bring lunch. And he'd tease her, argue with her, bawl her out and tell her he loved her. It made his day. . . . So, she grew up. And then Ted got on the phone to his friends and told them all about her—Jesus, he was so proud of her!—and with their help, he put together a fund that would help her get through college. *Goddammit, they had to help!*—that's what Ted said. He OWED her that!

IT WAS ALSO LATE IN LIFE, Ted found another love—in retrospect—for his opponents. While he was fighting them, he might have recognized his love of contest—but at the time, he wasn't blowing kisses their way.

The first who slipped into his new wider web of esteem were the fish. He'd always respected them—the bonefish for his wily quickness, the tarpon for his great graceful leaps, and the Atlantic salmon most of all—pound for pound the greatest fighter Ted knew. But it wasn't till his latter days—when there weren't so many fish anymore—that Ted stopped fighting, and tried to help them. He was always ready to offer his name, an appearance or a check, to save their habitat. In 1999, when the International Game Fish Association inducted him into its Hall of Fame—as the first-ever living member—Ted was near tears trying to express the joy these foes had brought him. He'd talk about them like gifted friends, with amazement and pride that he knew them. For example, he'd say: "Those damn tarpon . . . they'd grab a bucktail jig and WHOOOMM!—they'd jump, and take off." Two out of ten of 'em—that's how many Ted could reel in. Then he'd ask: "Do you know *anybody else* that held Ted Williams to a .200 average?"

In fact, Ted extended the love of his study to all the great game species. He might shout and argue through an afternoon with whoever happened to be in his living room. But once he'd commanded them to put into the VCR one of his *National Geographic* tapes, he was tautly silent (and if they meant to stay, they were, too). One time, on a visit with Breitbard to the San Diego Wild Animal Park, Ted enjoyed himself hugely as giraffes ate carrots from his hand, and he pitched heads of cabbage into the hippos' yawning mouths. But the high point for him was spotting a great, antlered buck grazing a hundred and fifty yards away. "Isn't that an Asian Père David buck?" Their guide about fell out of his seat.

"How'd you know that? There's only three I know about in captivity."

"CAPTIVITY HELL," Ted said. He saw 'em out there in Russia. "I'd say that bastard goes about four hundred sixty-five pounds."

Said the guide: "Well, I'll be damned. He weighed in at four-sixty-one."

Ted was the same about his baseball opponents—especially as they grew older: the attention they had required from him, and attention they had paid to frustrate him, was now fondness. Though strokes had left him partially paralyzed, Ted would not miss the opening of the Yogi Berra Museum in Upper Montclair, New Jersey. Why? Because the minute Ted shifted his feet six inches forward in the batter's box, Yogi would stand up, stop the pitcher and say: *What the hell's going on here?* "You couldn't put ANYTHING over on that goddamn Yogi." . . . In the same way, Ted was delighted when Phil Rizzuto was at last enshrined in the Cooperstown Hall of Fame. Of course, Ted had always liked Rizzuto—because "he was JUST A DAMN RUNT! But he played smart, see?—a SMART sonofabitch." (Rizzuto, for his part, used to tell the story of Ted sliding into second base, one day, then asking: "Hey! What're you doing for dinner? Why don't you and Cora come out with me?" Phil said he couldn't—Cora was in the hospital. And after the game, when Rizzuto got to her room, there was Ted looming over her hospital bed, with a rolled-up paper in his hands—showing her how HE hit the old apple. "Cora," Rizzuto said, "was scared to death.")

All the underdogs who made it had Ted's approbation, all the more when their handicaps were unjust. At his own induction into baseball's Hall of Fame—in 1966 his old foes, the writers, paid him the ultimate compliment by voting him in at their first opportunity—Ted used his moment in the spotlight of history to argue for enshrinement of Satchel Paige, Josh Gibson, and the other great players of the Negro Leagues, who never had a chance to show the wider world what they could do. (With the weight of his words, Paige and Gibson were inducted by the early 1970s, and others followed.) But that was consistent with Ted, too. Larry Doby, the American League's first black player, suffered scorn, insults and beanballs—just as Jackie Robinson did in the National League (they broke in the same year, 1947). As Doby recalls now, most big-time white players simply frosted him with the silent treatment—as, for instance, Joe DiMaggio, who would never say a word to Doby while they played, and *still* would never speak to him when they were both old men and Hall of Famers. But it wasn't that way at Fenway. Doby was on his first visit there, trotting toward his outfield post, when he stopped for his glove (in those days, players left them in the grass beyond the infield). "Hey! Congratulations." Doby looked up to see Ted Williams, on his way in from left field. "And good luck," Ted said.

On the subject of opponents, it would be well to spend a few words on *Ted's* relationship with Joe D. There was no one he'd rather beat. But Ted would never be small about a rivalry. After Ted's epic '41 season—the last anybody ever hit .400—when the writers voted the M.V.P. honor to DiMag (and his fifty-six-game streak), instead of Williams (and .406), Ted's comment was characteristically generous: "Well," he said, "it took the Big Guy to beat me." In retirement, Ted never caviled to say that DiMaggio was the greatest of their age. . . . But Joe could not reciprocate the kindness. While they played, one writer asked about Ted, and Joe said: "Best left-handed hitter I've seen." When the writer persisted—*But what about Williams as a man, as a player . . . you know, the whole rivalry?*—Joe said again: "Best left-handed hitter I've seen." In private, the Clipper was much less polite: "He throws like a broad," DiMag would say. "And he runs like a ruptured duck." When they were both up in years and supposed to be friendly—or at least act friendly—Joe never had much to say. Once, when they were at some affair, Joe got up to the microphone and offered a bit of backhanded tribute: he lamented that he'd never gone fishing with the great angler, Ted Williams. But Ted was ready for that. He shouted, right from his seat (he didn't need no stinkin' microphone): "Sonofabitch! I invited ya THREE TIMES.

YOU'D NEVER COME!" (Which was accurate, and also characteristic—for Ted would have fished Joe right out of the boat.)

The last opponents to be accorded Ted's love—well, at least he'd tolerate the good ones—were pitchers. Ted had, through decades, loudly and famously, branded them as *"non-athletes* . . . and STUPID! They ALWAYS gave you something to hit." But as he aged, even they looked better to him. He got to the point where he'd call a few of them friends—for instance, Eldon Auker, the old submariner. (He was even older than Ted—probably the last man who'd pitched in earnest to Babe Ruth.) Ted got so large about this that he'd even memorialize a few pitchers in the Ted Williams Museum and Hitters Hall of Fame. Of course, they couldn't get into the Hall—but he'd put up a plaque for them on the "Ted Williams Wall of Lifetime Achievement." Anyway, they'd come when he called. Any tribute from Ted was a pitcher's highest accolade. (One night in retirement, Whitey Ford was watching TV—an interview with the aged Ted Williams—and he named Whitey Ford as one of two pitchers who gave him trouble. As Ford recalled, "I jumped out of my lounge chair, I was so excited.") . . . At the annual induction ceremonies, most pitchers would include in their remarks some mention of Ted's well-known contempt. In 1999, it was the Cardinals' and Phillies' ace lefty, Steve Carlton, who had retired about a decade before—after twenty-four years of "non-athletics"—and more than four thousand strikeouts, three-hundred twenty-nine wins. . . . "Ted hated pitchers and he always thought they were stupid," Carlton told the crowd. "So I don't know why he's giving this award. But to the four thousand one hundred thirty-six *geniuses* who swung at my slider in the dirt—I thank you."

NOW THAT TED'S GONE, we can only hope and trust that he saved a little love for himself—especially for his Kid self—in the troublous and impassioned first half of his life. For in the service of his joke, Carlton may have come up with just the right word.

I think it was Einstein (Albert, the physicist—not Charles, who edited *The Fireside Book of Baseball*) who gave this definition of *genius*: "It is simply the capacity for taking infinite pains."

So what other word could we apply to Ted Williams—say, for instance, to Ted in his forties (already so accomplished at his first-chosen art)—who would lock himself away by night at his workbench, making his big hands into instruments of delicate creation, using monofilament, balsa, and feathers, to tie perfect imitations of God's insects—more and more perfect flies than any other man would tie—so he could, the next day, launch them with titanic technical prowess through the air, a hundred feet from his boat, on a fly-line so fine it would disappear even over sun-stark Florida flats, until every foot of his line was asoar, and the perfect fly would curl perfectly over the line's last six inches to settle on the water, as gently as God ever fed a fish lunch.

Or what should we say about the slightly younger Ted, who left the life he'd dreamed of, dutifully and for love of country, to face his fear—not a fear of dying, but fear that a guy who barely got through high school might not be able to master the avionics of an F-9 jet. But he did master them, in study and practice—he learned with the rigor of an engineer the mathematics of warring lift and drag (and learned it so well that still, as a half-blind old man, he could draw it from memory on an airline cocktail napkin, along with every working part of his jet engine); he learned to hear in the ram-roar of his plane the very top of a climb, the last instant to pull out of a dive (learned it so well that when he was sick in Korea, and couldn't hear at all, still he could fly by the sound in his mind); he learned when he loosed his bombs to use the jolting lift of his plane to bank and climb and get the hell away, he learned the turning tendencies of the rival Russian MiG, learned the way flak burst not at its apogee but slightly before . . . he made himself into a warrior pilot—because there were no pains he wouldn't take to learn.

And what else could we possibly say about the very young Ted—that handsome and headstrong, often heartsick lad in his twenties—who'd travel every winter to Kentucky, to choose by his own eye (the whitest ash, the tightest grain) the lumber for his own Louisville Sluggers at the factory of Hillerich & Bradsby . . . who, when those bats came, would haul them to the post office to make sure they were just the right weight . . . and come midsummer, he'd haul them all to the scales again, lest August over-weight them with a half-ounce of humidity.

Could there be any other word for a hitter who would envision the strike zone at the width of exactly seven baseballs—counting pitches on the corners, of course—and, at his six-foot-three, a height of exactly eleven balls . . . so, within that rectangle of seventy-seven balls, he could assign percentages to measure how well he would hit a pitch in each ball position . . . so he could choose a pitch in his Happy Zone—say, belt high in the middle of the plate, where he could hit .400 or better, instead of low and away, where the best he could hope for was .230 . . . and so he could teach a young hitter, with perfect precision and assurance, that if he swung at pitches just two inches *outside that zone,* he would increase the pitcher's target from four-point-two square feet to almost five-point-eight—an increase of thirty-seven per-cent. "Allow a pitcher that much of an advantage and you will be a .250 hitter."

Nothing was beyond or beneath Ted's notice—not even the dirt he stood on. Here, for example, is Ted with his coauthor, John Underwood, on the subject of batter's boxes. "Fans think they're all alike, and most batters probably do. They're all four feet by six, and they look alike. But it isn't so. I know for a fact the batter's box in Boston was a fraction higher in the back than in the front. I always felt I had a better hold with my back foot when I swung there. In Kansas City, I felt the box slanted the other way—I felt as if I were hitting uphill. I told the groundskeeper about it, and the next time we came into Kansas City it was level. I hit two home runs that day, and when the Kansas City manager learned what had happened he almost fired the groundskeeper."

You could call it a bent for science—but with Ted it wasn't for advance of man's knowledge, it was combat. Some people called it monomania—but with Ted it was serial (*multimania?*) in eager furtherance of everything he loved. I'd call it simply the capacity for taking infinite pains. Of if you prefer Lefty Carlton's analysis, we should take one more look at the line in the record book for Ted's third season—when he turned twenty-three years old:

He recorded four hundred fifty-six at bats.

He hit safely one hundred eighty-five times for a major-league-leading, history-making average of .406.

He disdained bad pitches and walked another hundred forty-five times, to lead both leagues again and raise his on-base average to .551—more than *half the time*, he succeeded at the hardest act in sports—which also led both leagues.

He hit more home runs (thirty-seven), scored more runs (one hundred thirty-five), and knocked in more runs (one hundred and forty-five) than any other man in major league baseball. . . .

And if you'd been lucky enough to watch every inning of every Red Sox game that year, 1941, you would have seen Ted strike out twenty-seven times—or about once a week.

IN 1991, the Red Sox mounted a grand celebration for the fiftieth anniversary of that season, and they brought Ted to Fenway again, drove him onto the field on the back of a golf cart—and to an endless standing ovation from the Boston fans. This kicked off a decade—his last—of the baseball nation bringing Ted back, so its citizens could show him love as they never had before. And right at the start, that first Fenway show, Ted signaled he was ready for a group-hug, too. Although he wasn't in uniform on the back of that cart, he dug into a pocket of his jacket and came forth with a Red Sox ballcap—so he could give the fans what he'd always denied them. He put the cap on his head, and then lifted it off, and twirled it around, waving it over his bare head, to the right-field stands, and left- —where the leather-lungs used to sit to boo him—and even toward that aerie above home plate, where a new generation of The Knights of the Keyboard were clacking away on their laptop computers.

In November that year, he was summoned to the White House—in company with Joe DiMaggio—to be honored not by the baseball nation, but America as a whole. The President, George Bush the Elder, awarded the old warriors the Medal of Freedom, the nation's highest civilian honor. Bush saluted Ted both as a "true champion" and a "twice-tested war hero." Ted's turn at the microphone was graceful and to the point: "I've always realized what a lucky guy I've been in my life. I was born in America. I was a Marine. I served my country. I'm very proud of that. I got to play baseball, had a chance to hit. I owe so very very much to this game that I love so much. And I want to thank you, Mr. President."

So it went on . . . Ted flew across the country to the All-Star Game in his hometown, San Diego. There he buttonholed the local star, Tony Gwynn, and bawled him out for the way he was hitting—"usin' a goddamn

TOOTHPICK for a bat!" At that point, Gwynn only had four batting titles to his credit. But Gwynn decided Ted was correct—after that, he hit with more power to right, instead of always slapping singles to the left side. "He turned my game around," Tony said. . . . Ted showed up in Boston, in a string-tie (the only sort of tie he would suffer—and that maybe twice in ten years), for a tuxedo and long-gown bash in his honor to benefit the Jimmy Fund. Ted made the date because it would raise money. (Two million!) But he really didn't want the fuss. He told the director of the fund: "Aw, you give me too much damn credit." . . . Ted sat in his house for an interview with CNN. Of course, he knew they were there because he'd be gone soon—he was eighty years old, couldn't walk worth a damn, and had to dab away saliva that bubbled unbidden from the corner of his mouth—but he could still wield the needle. As the interviewer that day, Leigh Montville, remembered in an eloquent tribute for *Sports Illustrated,* Ted finished the visit by expressing his opinion that he should have been offered some compensation. Ted demanded of Montville: WHO'S YOUR BOSS? . . .

"I said I had a lot of them," Montville wrote. "He asked who was the biggest boss, the boss of all bosses. I said I guessed Ted Turner was the biggest boss. . . .

" 'Well, you tell Ted Turner that Ted Ballgame would

like some remuneration, O.K.?' Williams said. 'Tell Ted that Ted would like something he could fold and put in his pocket. You know?' . . ."

The net result of Ted's ten-year grand tour was that we, his fans, were offered a series of snapshots—as Ted's storied body betrayed him, and the spirit that was his real greatness grew. It was a last gift from a born teacher. And the last view for most fans may have been the best.

That was in July 1999, at the last All-Star Game to be played at Fenway Park. (The old ballyard—like its greatest star, alas—was irreparably crumbling.) . . . It was after 8:30 P.M. east coast time. Once again, the Lords of Baseball had relegated the game itself to the wee hours—the pageant was the product. The All-Stars of the moment had been introduced, along with a gaggle of Hall of Famers who'd come to lend this Made-for-Fox broadcast the Good Housekeeping Seal of History . . . but then something real happened.

The green golf cart bearing the eighty-year-old Ted Williams nosed into view on the center-field warning track. And the fans in the packed grandstand rose with a roar. Ted had a white ballcap this time, which he waved as the cart puttered through the outfield, toward the pitcher's mound, where it stopped. There, the five biggest names in the game at the end of the century drew near—and then they hung back like boys. Ted could barely see, so the driver introduced them: Mark McGwire, Sammy Sosa, Tony Gwynn, Ken Griffey, Jr., and Cal Ripken, Jr. They all shook hands with the great man. Ted still hadn't gotten off his cart—he couldn't get off. The microphones picked up Ted asking McGwire if he could smell the singe of wood from his bat when he fouled one off—Ted said HE used to smell it. . . .

Off-mike, a Fox producer protested to the driver (Al Forester, a forty-five-year Fenway employee), "We're running late!" But as Forester recalled for the *Hartford Courant:* "I looked over my left shoulder and Nomar [the Sox shortstop, Nomar Garciaparra] was standing right there. I said, 'Nomar.' And Ted says, 'Where's Nomar?' . . ." (Ted LOVED that kid—saw him as a rookie and announced the boy had a swing like DiMaggio!) . . . So Nomar came over and talked to Ted. And then they all came in a flood—Joe Torre, manager for the American League, and all his players, and the National Leaguers and the Hall of Famers, too—Hank Aaron, Willie Mays and Bob Feller had to shove their way in . . . Ted was weeping with happiness—and they wouldn't leave him. The Foxies were half-mental and drenched in flop-sweat. They sent a protest to the commissioner. (Their show was late!) The P.A. announcer was enlisted, and his voice boomed over the field, asking the players to retreat—like a lifeguard trying to get the kids out of the pool. But they wouldn't leave. Half of them were crying, too. And half the people in the stands . . .

At last Ted was helped off his golf cart, and they aided, half-carried him, onto the mound, so he could throw out the first pitch. As Forester, the driver, recalled: "Carlton Fisk was the catcher. Ted said, 'Where is he?' The poor guy couldn't see."

So they pointed for Ted, to show where Fisk was. Tony Gwynn embraced Ted's weak left side, so he wouldn't fall as he threw. . . . And gamely, Ted reared back and let 'er rip—threw it straight to Fisk, on the fly. And it was a strike, too.

EVEN AFTER THE DOLEFUL DRUMBEAT of wire stories—Ted's pacemaker, the open heart surgery, the daily dialysis, the breathing tube—it was still a shock when Ted went . . . and a baleful bad day, July 5, 2002.

It was more than a day, for the death of Ted seemed to go on in slow motion, like a train wreck in the movies, or the fold-o by the Red Sox every August . . . that no one could stop, and it only grew uglier, louder with contention, pseudo-science jabber on TV, and newsprint sanctimony . . .

Well—I consoled myself—did you think he'd go QUIETLY?

Still, after a few days of TV chat-fest about poor Ted,

hanging by his frozen feet—his son, John Henry, had him stuck away in a cryogenic Frigidaire, supposedly (so Ted's elder daughter said) in hopes of selling his genes for future cloning . . . I was roundly depressed. It was the All-Star break, too—which didn't help: no real baseball at all.

I got a call from a friend, Mark Zwonitzer. He'd been my partner on a couple of books, and a couple of films, too.

"Hey, did you hear? The Florida Marlins just drafted Ted's D.N.A."

Only then, I recalled the first time I met Mark—he was a kid fact-checker for *Esquire,* who cleaned up my sloppiness in '86, on that first Ted Williams story. But now I just snarled at his joke: "Don't even say that."

He was silent for an instant, with the bane in my voice. But it turned out he remembered better than I did:

"Don't worry about him," he said. "In the year 2102, they'll thaw him out. And he'll sit right up and shout, 'What do you think of Ted Williams NOW?' "

With Mark McGwire on his right, and Tony Gwynn supporting Ted's weak left side, the grand old man threw out the first pitch—July 1999. (Reuters NewMedia Inc./CORBIS)

TED WILLIAMS'S
CAREER STATISTICS

ONE OF SEVENTEEN MEN in major-league history to come to bat three times in an inning (July 4, 1948).

One of five players to lead the majors in runs scored for three straight seasons, 1940–42, and again in 1946 after his return from World War II. The other four, by the way, were a nice group: Eddie Collins, Babe Ruth, Mickey Mantle, and Pete Rose.

Tied (with Babe Ruth and Reggie Jackson) for AL record with sixteen seasons of twenty or more home runs.

Tied (oddly, with John Olerud) for AL record for most intentional walks in a season thirty-three, in 1957—far behind the NL record of forty-five by Willie McCovey in 1969.

Williams, Theodore Samuel

(The Splendid Splinter, The Thumper)
B. Aug. 30, 1918, San Diego, Calif.

	G	AB	H	2B	3B	HR	HR %	R
1939 BOS A	149	565	185	44	11	31	5.5	131
1940	144	561	193	43	14	23	4.1	134
1941	143	456	185	33	3	37	8.1	135
1942	150	522	186	34	5	36	6.9	141
1946	150	514	176	37	8	38	7.4	142
1947	156	528	181	40	9	32	6.1	125
1948	137	509	188	44	3	25	4.9	124
1949	155	.566	194	39	3	43	7.6	150
1950	89	334	106	24	1	28	8.4	82
1951	148	531	169	28	4	30	5.6	109
1952	6	10	4	0	1	1	10.0	2
1953	37	91	37	6	0	13	14.3	17
1954	117	386	133	23	1	29	7.5	93
1955	98	320	114	21	3	28	8.8	77
1956	136	400	138	28	2	24	6.0	71
1957	132	420	163	28	1	38	9.0	96
1958	129	411	135	23	2	26	6.3	81
1959	103	272	69	15	0	10	3.7	32
1960	113	310	98	15	0	29	9.4	56
19 yrs.	2292	7706	2654	525	71	521 10th	6.8 5th	1798
World Series								
1946 BOS A	7	25	5	0	0	0	0.0	2

Holds a host of All-Star Game records (through 2001):
Most hits, runs, HRs, and RBIs in a game (four, four, two,
five respectively—all in 1946; two other players have had
four hits, four others have had two HRs); most total bases
in a game (ten, in '46 of course); tied with Brooks Robinson

112

Manager 1969–72. Hall of Fame 1966.
BL   TR   6'3"   205 lbs.

RBI	BB	SO	SB	BA	SA	Pinch Hit AB	H	G by POS
145	107	64	2	.327	.609	0	0	OF-149
113	96	54	4	.344	.594	0	0	OF-143, P-1
120	145	27	2	.406	.735	9	3	OF-133
137	145	51	3	.356	.648	0	0	OF-150
123	156	44	0	.342	.667	0	0	OF-150
114	162	47	0	.343	.634	0	0	OF-156
127	126	41	4	.369	.615	2	0	OF-134
159	162	48	1	.343	.650	0	0	OF-155
97	82	21	3	.317	.647	1	1	OF-86
126	144	45	1	.318	.556	0	0	OF-147
3	2	2	0	.400	.900	4	1	OF-2
34	19	10	0	.407	.901	10	2	OF-26
89	136	32	0	.345	.635	4	2	OF-115
83	91	24	2	.356	.703	2	1	OF-93
82	102	39	0	.345	.605	20	5	OF-110
87	119	43	0	.388	.731	5	3	OF-125
85	98	49	1	.328	.584	11	3	OF-114
43	52	27	0	.254	.419	24	11	OF-76
72	75	41	1	.316	.645	19	1	OF-87
1839 10th	2019 2nd	709	24	.344 6th	.634 2nd	111	33	OF-2151, P-1
1	5	5	0	.200	.200	0	0	OF-7

and Cal Ripken for AL mark for most All-Star Game appearances, eighteen; AL mark for most career runs scored (ten, way behind the NL leader, Willie Mays, who had twenty), as well as most hits, extra-base hits, total bases, HRs, walks, and RBIs (the last two, major-league leads).

113

Batting titles separated by the most years—1941 and 1958.

Not only the oldest man to win the batting title (thirty-nine in 1958), Williams is also the second oldest (thirty-eight in 1957).

Williams had the highest BB/K ratio for any hitter with 200 HR.

He was the oldest man to "decimalize" his age—.388 at age thirty-eight. (No one else older than thirty-six has done this.)

Williams led the league in walks and RBIs in the same season three times—an interesting and unlikely combination. Ruth did it five times; no one else did it more than twice.

Ted hit home runs in four consecutive at bats, over five games, in September 1957. Here's how:

> 9/17: pinch-hit HR
> 9/18: pinch-hit, drew a walk
> 9/20: pinch-hit HR
> 9/21: four plate appearances: BB, HR, BB, BB
> 9/22: BB, HR, 1B . . .

ABOUT THE AUTHOR

RICHARD BEN CRAMER is the author of the best-selling *Joe DiMaggio: The Hero's Life* and *What It Takes: The Way to the White House*. He has written for *Esquire, Rolling Stone, The New York Times Magazine, Time,* and *Newsweek*. In 1979, he won a Pulitzer Prize for his dispatches from the Middle East. He lives on Maryland's eastern shore with his wife and daughter.